Pets and Other Animals

Pets and Other Animals

A Supplement to Childcraft—The How and Why Library

World Book, Inc.
a Scott Fetzer company
Chicago   London   Sydney   Toronto

World Book, Inc.
525 W. Monroe
Chicago, IL 60661

ISBN 0-7166-0692-5
Library of Congress Catalog Card No. 65-25105

Printed in the United States of America

Contents

Preface

It's nice to cuddle up with a kitten...or romp with a puppy... or stroke a bunny's silky, soft fur... or giggle as a frog gobbles a bug. If you have a pet of your own, you know how much joy it brings you. But your pet needs a lot of care and attention in return. *Pets and Other Animals* tells you what you need to know to keep your pet healthy and happy.

But maybe you don't own a pet. This book also shows you how to "have a pet" without keeping an animal in a cage, a box, or a tank. You can observe a spider spinning its web, or put food out for the birds in your neighborhood. Or you can help care for a friend's or relative's pet.

This book is full of information about all kinds of pets—pets that people own and "wild pets" that run, swim, crawl, or fly free. So take your dog for a walk, make a salad for your hamster, or watch a squirrel bury an acorn. You'll soon find many ways to be a friend to an animal!

True Blue
Buddies

A Dog's Best Friend—You!

We can learn a lot from Nellie, the proud mother of four handsome puppies.

"When my puppies were born, I fed them and kept them warm, safe, and clean. Soon, they will go to new homes. Each will need a friend to care for it. So if you want to be the very best friend a dog could have, here's what to do!"

Pamper your puppy. Before you bring your new puppy home, make sure you have prepared a comfortable puppy home. A cardboard box or a cage that is big enough for the puppy to stretch in makes a fine bed. Line the box or cage with soft cushions or blankets. Put newspapers under and around the bed until the puppy is housetrained. Place toys in the bed, and dishes for food and water nearby.

Pay attention to your puppy's feelings. Puppies have ways of showing you what they like and don't like. Talk to your puppy often, but try not to shout. Don't cuddle your puppy so tightly that it squirms uncomfortably. And never, ever poke or tease it.

Puppies may need as many as four small meals every day. Puppies also need a diet high in *protein,* a substance that helps the puppy grow. Most puppy foods that you can buy in a store provide this extra protein. You may also add healthy table scraps, such as egg, cottage cheese,

or lean meat, to your puppy's store-bought food to make sure it gets the protein it needs.

Take your new puppy to see a veterinarian within a week after you have brought it home. The veterinarian will check the puppy's general health and give it *vaccinations,* which are shots that help protect your puppy from serious diseases. Also, be sure to ask the vet for bathing and brushing instructions.

Pet Pointer

A grown-up dog can be a great new family pet. Animal shelters are full of adult dogs that need good homes. Just make sure you choose a healthy, alert, friendly dog.

You'll need to teach your puppy to behave well indoors and to get along with other people. It also must learn to tell you when it needs to go outside to the bathroom. Puppies do not need treats to learn tricks. The more you work with your pup, the more it will learn. Patiently show it what to do over and over again, and say "Good dog!" when it catches on. And when your puppy makes a mistake, a firm "No!" is all that's needed. Never punish it by shouting, handling it roughly, or spanking it.

Pet Pointer

Teaching a New Dog New Tricks

Puppies and dogs need to learn five basic commands. This is called *obedience training*.

SIT Press gently on your dog's backside with one hand and pull up slightly on its leash with the other while repeating the command "Sit."

DOWN When your dog is sitting, hold its front legs and gently lower it until it is lying down. Say "Down" at the same time.

At about one year of age, a dog is full-grown. Your puppy's stubby face has taken on a grown-up look. Your dog can run faster and leap higher than ever. It knows more commands and tricks and learns new ones more quickly. But your dog still depends on you for its health and happiness.

Dogs like to follow a regular schedule. So try to feed and walk your dog at about the same time every day. A grown-up dog needs

HEEL When your dog pulls ahead or falls behind, give the leash a quick tug and say "Heel," until the dog is by your side.

STAY Say "Stay" and hold one hand flat in front of your dog's face as you walk away backwards. If the dog moves, say "No, sit, stay." Then press it back into place.

COME After your dog has learned to stay, walk away from it and then call "Come."

Remember: The better a dog obeys, the better you can protect it. Can you think how the command "stay" could save a dog's life?

"What a shiny coat! What good manners! You have taken excellent care of your puppy and given it a great start in life. Keep up the good work!"

one or, better, two meals and one or two long or fast-paced walks per day.

Many dogs, especially long-haired ones, need daily combing or brushing, called *grooming*. If you learn to comb and brush your dog gently, it will soon begin to love the attention. And it will look and feel great! Grooming sessions are also a good time to check for fleas, ticks, or other problems, such as dandruff or nails that have grown too long. A veterinarian can correct most of these problems.

Visits to the veterinarian are an important part of dog care. Your healthy dog needs a checkup once a year, without fail. You will be surprised how much your dog's checkup reminds you of your own checkup! The doctor looks in your dog's ears, eyes, nose, and throat. The veterinarian takes its temperature and pulse, listens to its heart and lungs with a stethoscope, and gives it *booster shots* to keep the vaccinations working.

The veterinarian will explain how to tell if your dog is ill. Signs include tiredness, fever, runny eyes, runny nose, coughing, smelly ears, strange body movements, vomiting or diarrhea, and constant chewing or scratching. Always have the veterinarian's phone number on hand in case of accident or illness.

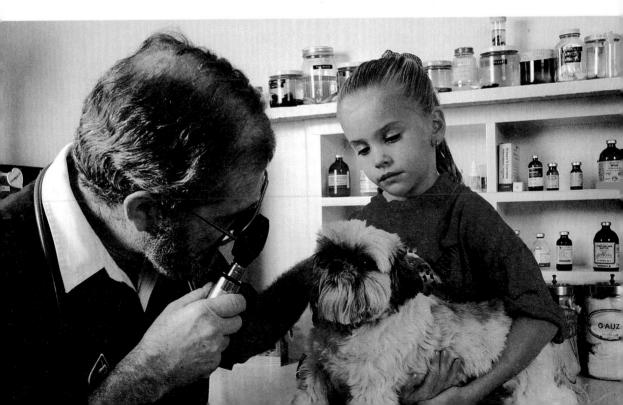

Adventures in Dog Walking

Mr. and Mrs. Ortega had just moved to the neighborhood with their beautiful collie. Molly Martin knocked on their door. "Hi. I'm here to offer my services as a dog walker," she stated. "I walk dogs for several families on the block. Every day, rain or shine. My card...."

"I'm glad to meet you," Mr. Ortega answered. "And here's our dear Silkie."

"Pretty Silkie," Molly murmured as she stroked the dog's long fur. "How are you today?" Silkie wagged her tail. "I treat my dogs like friends," Molly explained. "Would you like to go on a test walk?"

The four set off. "Silkie likes to have her walk at four o'clock every afternoon," said Mrs. Ortega.

"No problem," replied Molly. "I make up a schedule for all my dogs, and I never keep them waiting."

"Would you know what to do in an emergency?" asked Mr. Ortega.

"I'll always have your veterinarian's phone number with me," Molly answered confidently. Suddenly, a dog across the street barked excitedly. Silkie tried to drag Molly toward the misbehaving dog.

"Are you strong enough to hold her?" Mrs. Ortega asked with a worried frown.

Molly tugged the leash and pulled a doggie treat from her jacket. "Come, Silkie," she said firmly. Silkie scampered after her.

"You're the best, Molly!" Mr. Ortega exclaimed. "Can you start tomorrow?"

"I think she's already started," said Mrs. Ortega, and they all laughed.

Good Show!

Dog shows are lively and fun to attend, even if you don't have a dog. Rows and rows of stalls and cages contain every kind of dog you can imagine. Owners and handlers wearing armbands for identification hurry to and fro, exercising their dogs or signing up for events. At some stalls, owners prepare their dogs for competition. They brush them, check their teeth, or stroke them to keep them calm. In other stalls, perfectly groomed dogs nap contentedly, waiting for their turn to be judged.

At a dog show, you may see some of the world's most unusual dogs. Instead of barking, the basenji makes a sound that resembles yodeling. The shar-pei has a wrinkled face that makes it look like a wise old person. You also may admire elegant Afghan hounds with silky hair trailing the ground, tiny *toy* dogs, such as the Chihuahua and Pekingese, and such giants of the dog world as the great Dane and Irish wolfhound.

A championship show is a little like a beauty contest for purebred dogs. A champion dog must be as close as possible to the perfect size, color or colors, and shape for its breed.

Getting a whisker trim is all in a day's work as an English bulldog and its trainer get ready for competition.

Dogs compete in open areas called *rings.* In one ring, dogs pose for judges. This is often called *stacking.* Owners place their dogs in a standing posture with their feet firmly planted and their heads held high. The dogs are judged according to how good they look and how well they stay in the stacking position.

In another ring, the judges watch the dogs move. This part of the competition is called *gaiting.* It is named for a dog's *gait,* which is the way it walks. In this competition, dogs walk or trot on a leash in a variety of patterns—triangular, T-shaped, L-shaped, and straight line.

Many dogs earn points at the dog show, and some win awards. The award "Best of Breed" is given to the dog that,

Poodles that compete in dog shows have fluffy, fancy haircuts, just like these standard poodles. Here a judge is examining the dogs in the part of the show called the *stacking competition.*

In obedience trials, dogs can win awards for being the most well behaved. These dogs are performing the "long sit and stay." They are not allowed to move until their trainers give them the command.

in the judges' opinion, is the most perfect example of each breed. These dogs continue to compete until one is chosen "Best in Show."

Years of training and hard work have paid off for today's winners. Some of them now can add a new title before their names—the letters *Ch.* This title stands for "Champion." A dog earns the right to be called "Champion" by winning titles in several dog shows.

A dog show may include other special events, too. *Obedience trials* measure dogs' skills in following such basic commands as "heel," "sit," and "stay." *Field trials* test hunting and tracking skills. They are held in a wooded area instead of an arena.

Pet Words to Know

A **purebred** is a dog that has ancestors of the same breed going back several generations.

A **mongrel** is a mixed-breed dog, or mutt—one that is not a purebred. To say that a dog is a mongrel does not mean that it's dirty, ill-behaved, or unloved.

A **pedigree** is a written record of a dog's ancestors.

Why Does a Dog?

Why does a dog wag its tail?

People often think that when a dog wags its tail, it's always saying, "I'm happy!" But a dog can wag its tail in different ways to say different things, such as "Hello," or "I'm top dog!"

Why does a dog pant?

Sometimes a dog breathes hard with its tongue hanging out. It is not out of breath or afraid. It's just panting. Panting is a dog's "air conditioning." The air cools the dog inside and out.

Why is a dog's nose wet?

A cold, wet nose is usually a sign of a healthy dog. Dogs release moisture through their noses and mouths to cool themselves. A dry, chapped nose that stays warm might mean the dog has a fever and needs to see a veterinarian.

How fast can the fastest dog run?

Greyhounds, sleek and trim racing dogs, have been clocked in races at more than forty miles (64 kilometers) an hour. That's faster than a race horse!

Pet Pointer

If an unfamiliar dog approaches you, don't run away. Running away may excite the dog, and it may chase you and even bite you. Instead, stand still, and without staring at the dog, speak quietly to it. If it comes closer, allow it to sniff you, then back away slowly.

Pet Pointer

Learn Dog Language

Dogs use body language to tell you what they want and how they feel. Here is a dog "vocabulary list."

"I'd like some food, please."

"Let's play!"

What does a dog do if it senses danger?

When dogs feel threatened, their bodies "go on alert." Their ears prick up or forward, their legs straighten, their tails stand straight up or out, and their eyes stare intently. Trained dogs alert when their masters are threatened, too.

Why does a dog sniff the ground?

Dogs pick up scents of other dogs, animals, and people this way. Even if the scents are all mixed up by wind or rain, dogs can tell them apart. When dogs walk, their paws leave a scent that other dogs can follow.

"I need to go to the bathroom."
or
"I want to go for a walk."

"I'm sorry."

How does a rabid dog act?

A rabid dog has *rabies,* a deadly disease. This disease causes a dog to growl and often drool. Rabid dogs also have a strange, crooked walk. They seem fearless and crazy, and were once called "mad dogs." *Mad* is another word for crazy. If you think a dog has rabies, do not go near it. Instead, go indoors and call the police or animal control authorities to report it.

What does a dog like to do most?

Please its master. Most dogs try hard to be good pets.

Happy Homecoming

It was bedtime, and Kyle wrote in his journal. "Today is the saddest day of my life. Flash is missing, and it's all my fault! I went bike riding this afternoon. When I got back home, I was so hot and thirsty I went straight for the hose for a drink. I didn't realize I hadn't closed the gate. I'm not even sure when she escaped."

That afternoon, right after Flash disappeared, Mom and Dad tried to make

Kyle feel better. "No one is perfect," Mom said. "Don't blame yourself."

"But what if she never comes back?" Kyle cried.

"We'll just have to make sure she does," said Dad.

Dad called the local paper to place a lost dog notice, and Mom helped Kyle make posters with Flash's picture to put up in the neighborhood.

"Maybe we should ask the mail carrier and the garbage collectors whether they've seen Flash," Kyle suggested.

"Good idea," said Mom. "And I'll call all the veterinary hospitals and animal shelters in the area and leave Flash's description."

"Would it help if we told them Flash's dog tag numbers?" Kyle asked.

"Sure would," Dad said. "But," he added sadly, "I never wrote them down."

"I did!" Kyle exclaimed. Kyle had been so excited when Flash had first come to

Pet Pointer

The identifying numbers on rabies tags and dog licenses are kept on record at the animal control department where you live. These numbers can help identify your dog if it is lost and brought to a shelter. Get a rabies tag at the veterinarian's office when your dog has its rabies shots. Your local animal control office or your veterinarian can tell you how to apply for a dog license.

live with the family. He had written down almost everything about her—even her tag numbers—in his journal.

Kyle was so worried about Flash that he tossed and turned all night. "Where is she?" he wondered. "Is she warm? Does she have enough to eat?"

The next day went by slowly. The family moped all evening. Suddenly, the phone rang. Everyone jumped. "Yes.... Yes!" Kyle heard his mother say. "We'll be right down!"

"Flash?" Kyle asked hopefully.

"Flash," Mom answered with a grin.

The moment Flash saw Kyle, she wagged her tail so hard that it looked like a blur. Kyle hugged Flash as hard as he could and thought he'd never let go.

The man at the animal shelter smiled. The happy reunion made him feel good, too. He told Kyle and his parents that a farmer had found Flash romping in his pasture with his own two dogs. It was late in the evening. So the farmer fed Flash and let her sleep in the barn. He called the shelter the next day and reported the numbers on the dog tags.

"We told him the numbers on her tags matched the ones you had given us," he told them. "And he offered to bring her down to the shelter right away. We phoned you in the meantime."

"The nice farmer didn't even leave his name," wrote Kyle that night. "I guess we'll never meet him. But he's a real friend. I'll never forget him."

"The Flying Dog"

He streaks across the ground fast as lightning, leaps, and catches spinning flying discs in midair! No wonder this terrier-beagle from Phoenix, Arizona, is named Air Major.

According to his trainer, Bill Watters, Air Major showed skill at leaping and catching as a pup. So Watters taught him special tricks. In a trick called the "back vault," Air Major springs from the ground to Watters' shoulders and then high into the air to catch a flying disc. Watters and Air Major have competed in five world championships. Air Major performs for live audiences across the United States and has appeared often on TV.

Watters and Air Major have worked hard to become the best. They share what they know about setting and achieving goals in special presentations at elementary schools.

Henry's Hall of Fame

Welcome, people, to the Dogs' Hall of Fame. I'm Bloodhound Henry, your guide. We're taking this tour to show our appreciation for the many ways dogs contribute to human life.

Rock painting

Here is our first exhibit, an unnamed dog—one of the earliest dogs to befriend ancient people. We are not sure exactly what these age-old companions looked like. But cave and rock paintings thousands of years old show that dogs helped early humans to survive.

Sled dogs

Now, please step up and view the sled dog, represented here by the Siberian husky. (Some people consider them handsome—but look at those short ears!) Life in the icy lands of the north would have been impossible without such dogs.

Imagine that you are surrounded by a howling blizzard. You can see nothing in the fierce whiteness. Could you trek for miles pulling a sled loaded with supplies? Probably not by yourself. You'd need the help of the husky or one of its cousins, the Alaskan malamute and the Samoyed.

Airedale

Farmers and herders have depended on dogs for thousands of years. Here is the terrier, valued for its skill in killing rats and other pests. Herding dogs, such as the collie, the Old English sheepdog, and the German shepherd, have been tending sheep, goats, and cattle for hundreds of years.

Dogs also have earned their keep by helping hunters. Pointers, setters, and hounds locate game with their keen eyesight and sense of smell. Spaniels scare birds out of hiding. And retrievers gained their title because they *retrieve,* or bring back, game birds that have been shot.

Now let us turn to the Search and Rescue, or SAR, breeds. Here we see a German shepherd searching for survivors in a burned building. St. Bernards, Labrador retrievers, and my kin, the noble bloodhounds, serve as SAR dogs as well. (The others may be brave enough. But unfortunately, they lack the handsome wrinkles that adorn my

earch and rescue dog

It's a Pet Fact

Every year since 1954, a large U.S. pet food company has named a Dog Hero of the Year for a special act of bravery. The dogs that have won this award have saved the lives of many people and even other animals, overcoming such dangers as fires, speeding traffic, wild animal attacks, and fast-flowing rivers.

breed.) Through history, SAR dogs have rescued people from fires, earthquakes, floods, avalanches, and other disasters. Experts have estimated that SAR dogs' sense of smell is a million or more times keener than a human's. They can follow a person's scent for many miles. In many situations, one SAR dog and its handler can do the work of thirty rescuers.

Now follow me for a tour of the Guide and Companion Dog Wing. Here we honor dogs who unselfishly help people in special ways:

Seeing eye dogs act as eyes for the blind. They guide and protect their owners in traffic and other situations that are difficult for blind people.

Hearing ear dogs help the hearing-impaired. They alert their owners to everyday sounds, such as doorbells, and to danger signals, such as smoke alarms or sirens. Strays often make good hearing ear dogs when they are properly trained.

Seeing eye dog

Aid dog

People in wheelchairs find true friends in aid dogs. These dogs do the chores their masters cannot do. They provide protection, as well.

Therapy dogs work with their trainers to brighten the lives of patients in nursing homes and hospitals. Ill and elderly patients are often lonely. They feel better after petting and cuddling these dogs.

And finally, we honor Everydog. We do not know this dog's name, but it is every dog who has loyally served its master. It may not do anything special. But to its family, it's still a hero. Perhaps it's your dog!

·EVERYDOG·

Cats, Cats, Cats

Grandma Lily, and most other Siamese cats for that matter, cannot stop chattering. What a loud voice she has! But what a show cat she is! Look at those pretty dark brown points.

Grandpa Shabriar, a Persian, is one of the family's oldest long-haired cats. Long ago, a few cats had naturally long hair. Cat lovers spent years breeding more of these cats with beautiful coats. Owners of Persian cats have to brush out the tangles daily.

Great-Aunt Conchita, Grandpa's sister, is an odd-eyed white Persian. Study her picture closely. You will see that she has a blue eye and a copper-colored one.

Aunt Ling certainly has star quality. All Himalayans do, what with their Siamese coloring and luxuriously long fur. But imagine how hard she works to groom herself!

Pet Word to Know

Points are parts of a cat, including the face, ears, legs, feet, and tail, that have a different color than the rest of the body.

Grandma Scheherazade is a Turkish Angora. Angoras look a lot like Persians, but Persians have flatter faces. Early Angoras probably came from Turkey. They were named after a Turkish city that is now called Ankara.

Great-Uncle Alex, like Grandma Lily, is from the shorthaired side of the family. Like every other Abyssinian, he is a wonderful stalker and jumper.

Cousin Galina is called a Russian blue. The earliest Russian blues most likely came either from northern Russia or Scandinavia.

Louie the Rex is a newcomer to the family. The first Rexes, or curly-haired cats, arrived on the scene in about 1950. But curly hair isn't their only claim to fame. Rexes run faster and leap farther than most other cats.

Sumi comes from faraway Japan. Americans call her a Japanese bobtail. The daredevil of the family, Sumi and others of her breed actually love to swim.

What's different about Max the Manx? Take a second look. Manx cats have no tails, or very short ones. And—weird but true—they have a rabbitlike hop when they walk. The earliest Manxes came from the Isle of Man, between England and Ireland.

Cousin Seth lives closer to home. He belongs to the Maine coon breed, which includes some of the biggest cats in the world. Huge, isn't he? I bet his owners hitch him up to their sleigh each winter. Ha! Ha! Only kidding, Seth.

Here I am! After seeing pictures of my family, you may have guessed that I am a mixed breed. Actually, I have inherited the best traits from all my relatives, don't you think so?

Cat at Work

Casimir begins his day with a stretch. Then he pads into the kitchen to greet Mrs. Petrowski, his owner, with his upright tail waving gently. This tells her that he is glad to see her and his breakfast.

After eating, Casimir starts his rounds. First, he rubs his head against Mrs. Petrowski. Then he presses it against the table legs and chairs. Casimir is releasing scent markers. Their odor lets other cats know where he has been and how long ago he was there. When Casimir passes through a territory, he leaves scent markers along the way.

Once outdoors, Casimir pauses to listen. He slinks toward a rustling noise. Then he spies a mouse scurrying into a shed. Casimir darts after it. Inside, the shed is dark. Casimir can see far better in dim light than a person can, but he needs some light to see his way around. However, to feel his way around, Casimir needs only his whiskers.

Casimir's whiskers send messages to his brain in the same way that your fingers send messages to your brain. The whiskers on his upper lip tell him if a space is wide enough to fit through. The whiskers on his chin help him feel things on the ground. And the whiskers on his forelegs tell him if what he has caught is about to escape.

Casimir is a good mouser. His senses of sight, hearing, and touch help him make short work of the mouse in the shed.

Later, Casimir sits in the sun licking himself. The saliva on his tongue cools him off and cleans his fur. The bristles on his tongue comb out dirt and loose hairs.

Suddenly, a dog charges out from the next yard. Casimir arches his back. The fur on his tail puffs out, making the tail look twice its size. He puts out his claws. The cat's whole body says, "Don't mess with me."

But this dog doesn't frighten easily—
and the closer it comes, the bigger it
looks. In a wink, Casimir changes his
mind about attacking and uses his claws
to climb a nearby tree. Then he *retracts*,
or draws in, the claws. (Retracting the
claws keeps them sharp, and Casimir
may need sharp claws yet.) He uses his
tail for balance as he walks out on a limb
to wait. The dog seems to take forever to
go away.

When the coast is finally clear,
Casimir sizes up his situation. Like a

person but unlike a dog or a mouse, Casimir has eyes in the front of his face. They help him judge distances. He decides that he is close enough to the ground to jump.

Casimir's flexible backbone curves into an arch. His legs absorb some of the shock as he lands on all four feet. But even if Casimir had fallen, his "body righting reflex" would make certain he is upright. A natural balancing device inside his ear helps him stay that way.

Bones intact, Casimir strolls home. Mrs. Petrowski meets him with a saucer of cat food. As Casimir licks the saucer clean, Mrs. Petrowski scratches him and says: "Ah, what a life! Being a cat is good work if you can get it, eh, Casimir?" Casimir purrs in reply. Then he curls up and takes a nap.

Noble Companions

When cat lovers today say they "worship" their pets, they don't really mean that they think their cats are gods. But early Egyptians—some of the first cat lovers—may have believed that. At the very least, the Egyptians thought that cats were special to their gods and goddesses.

We know this because more than 2,400 years ago Herodotus, a Greek historian, wrote about an Egyptian goddess, Bastet. Bastet had a cat's head and a woman's body. Countless cats roamed her temple, and a major duty of the temple priests was to feed these cats.

When a cat died, the priests of Bastet mummified it just as the *pharaohs*, or Egyptian kings, were mummified. They wrapped the body of the dead cat in cloth. If a cat belonged to the temple or to a rich owner, its face was covered with a sculpted mask, and the cat mummy was placed in a cat-shaped coffin. Clearly, dead or alive, cats were precious to the early Egyptians.

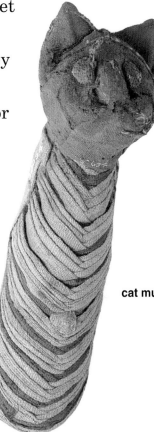

cat mummy

Even Egyptian law made clear how highly the people valued cats. It commanded that anyone who killed a cat be put to death.

Egyptians were not the only people to regard cats highly. A legend tells that the prophet Muhammad, who lived more than a thousand years ago, loved his cat, Meuzza, very dearly. One day, when he was wearing his favorite robe, she fell asleep on the sleeve. If he moved, he would wake her. Not wanting to disturb her, he cut off the sleeve of the robe and left her to finish her nap.

For many centuries, the Siamese also had special cat traditions. One of their legends tells that the shadowy patches of fur on a Siamese cat's neck are the dark thumbprints of gods who picked up the cat to admire it.

Siamese cats were considered royal. They lived only in the households of the royal family and very wealthy families, and in Buddhist temples. In 1884, to honor the British consul-general, the king of Siam (now Thailand) presented him with a pair of Siamese cats!

People in many lands associated cats with power and mystery. In ancient times, the Chinese gave thanks to a cat god for protecting their crops from rats. People in Ghana long ago thought that a person's spirit entered a cat's body when

It's a Pet Fact

In Japan, cats are considered good luck. Many shop owners place a figure of a Japanese bobtail with its paw raised in greeting in the window or door of their stores. It is supposed to bring customers to the shop.

the person died. In Tokyo, in the 1700's, the Japanese built a temple dedicated to the cat. It still stands, surrounded by a cat cemetery.

Today, the idea of cats as supernatural beings seems odd. But we can almost understand it when we watch the knowing eyes and surefooted, graceful movements of the cats around us.

Featured Creature

You have followed Alice around all day.
Now you hear her talking just up the way.
She's chatting to someone in a tree,
But not much of the creature can you see—
No eyes, no ears, no nose, no chin.
All you spy is a toothy grin.
To whom is she talking? Can you say?
Quick—the grin is fading away!

Answer: the Cheshire Cat

The Purr-fect Cat Owners

"Meow, meow, meooooow, meow, meow, meow, meooooow."

The three friends paused in their singing to lick their tails. Usually the tabbies sat quietly, listening for mice or the dog next door. But tonight they felt chatty. Soon Blanche, the tiger-striped cat, began telling her friends about her home life.

"You girls ought to see the nice place I have," Blanche said. "My bed is in the sunniest spot of the house. Some days I lie for hours and soak up the rays. On cloudy days, though, I nap on top of the TV, where it's warm. My owners let me stay there as long as I want."

"Hoo, boy!" said Martine, the brown tabby. "Cloudy days remind me of how I hate being caught in the rain. Nothing is worse than wet fur. So my owners put a cat door in the back of the house. With a flip of the flap, I'm inside before that first raindrop falls."

It's a Pet Fact

A cat can purr because it has a set of "false vocal cords" as well as the vocal cords it uses to meow. When the cat is happy and relaxed, its breath makes the false vocal cords vibrate with a rumbling, purring sound.

"Well, I can think of something worse than wet fur," Giselle, the silver tabby, chimed in. "It's a dirty litter box. Luckily, my owners scoop out the soiled litter and add fresh litter every day. Once a week, they wash the box with hot water. Using that box is a pleasure."

"For pure pleasure," Blanche spoke up, "try a taste of people food once in a while. Eating at the same time that my owners do feels pleasant, too. It's like being part of the family, you know?"

"Yes," Martine agreed. "I also like being around people. I especially enjoy having them fuss over me and give me toys."

"My best
gift ever was my
scratching post,"
Giselle said. "It keeps my
claws sharp and saves wear
and tear on my owners'
curtains."

"Can you imagine the yelling if you
tore up their sofa?" Blanche commented.
"Yelling makes me jumpy. Thank
goodness my owners talk in quiet,
friendly tones."

"Well, I hope singing doesn't make our
people jumpy," Martine joked, "because I
feel a song coming on. Care to join me?
Meow, meow, meoooooow...."

Puff at Play

Pet Pointer

A kitten should be picked up with both hands. Slide one hand under its chest and use the other to support its hind legs.

Here I am, fearless Puff, ready to take on any fish, bird, or mouse foolish enough to cross my path.

What is that silvery thing? It must be a salmon. It's strange that it swims on the floor and not in the water. No matter. Its time is up. Puff the master fishercat is on the job.

I will just lie and wait until it swims past. Come here, fishy-fishy. Quickly I slip my paw under the little guppy and flip the fish right out over my head.

What is this? The fish has a string tied to its tail. Well, it's still lunch, isn't it? Ptui! It tastes like a candy wrapper.

I was fooled once, but I may get a second chance. Look at that fluttering blue jay. This time I have to depend on my expert bird-catching skills.

The poor bird probably has no idea of the danger nearby. That's because

I'm such a good stalker. I sneak up on my prey ever so quietly.

The unsuspecting tweeter is perching on the chair. So I pounce. Drat! The bird flies up into the air. I leap and swipe at it with both front paws at once. There, I've captured it. Now to take a bite of my high-flying meal.

Say, this bird is not very meaty. In fact, it seems to be no bird at all. It's a piece of cloth. Still, I did a great job of catching it.

Wow! I've found a cave. Is anything inside, I wonder? Hmmm.

It looks as if a mouse lives here, and he appears to be sleeping. Slowly I pull my hind legs under my body. I leap forward and grab with my front paws. Got him!

I guess I'll go and show my catch to my owner. She will be so proud.

She doesn't seem very surprised. Probably she takes it for granted that I am a deadly hunter. Well, who can blame her? I always get my mouse.

Pet Project

Cat Mouse Toy

Things You Need:

- scissors
- marker
- two yards of yarn
- small paper clip
  or large yarn needle
- one-hole punch
- piece of felt at least 8"
  (20 centimeters) square
- tissue wrapping paper
- jingle bell

Here's a toy you can make for a cat you know or own.

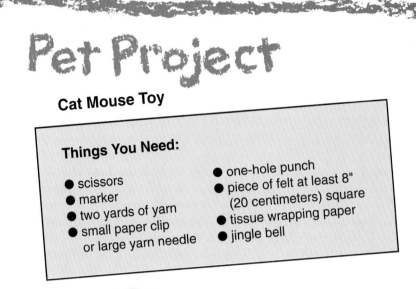

1. Place a sheet of tissue paper over the mouse toy patterns on pages 68-69. Trace the outline of the body. Mark the stitching holes and the slits for the ears. Trace the ear shape.

2. Pin the tissue patterns for the body and the ears on the felt. Cut the felt around each pattern.

3. Punch out the stitching holes through the marks on the tissue. Carefully cut the slits for the ears. Remove the tissue you used for tracing. Fold the mouse body in half, lining up the stitching holes. Slip the earpiece through the slits, so that one mouse ear sticks out on each side of the body.

4. Straighten the paper clip and bend a hook at the end to hold the yarn. Or, use a large yarn needle.

5. Ask someone to help with sewing if you need it. Thread the paper clip or needle with the piece of yarn. Tie a large knot in the end of the yarn.

6. Lace the mouse through the holes you punched in the felt. Start at the nose and stop before you reach the tail, leaving a small opening.

7. Stuff the mouse with tissue paper through the opening you left. Then finish lacing the mouse. After you make the last stitch, knot the yarn at the end of the mouse's body. Leave a piece of yarn as long as your hand for the tail. Then cut the yarn.

8. If you have a jingle bell, thread your needle with a short piece of yarn. Thread the yarn through the bell and the mouse's nose. Tie a double knot. Now it's time to play. Watch as your favorite cat stalks the mouse and crinkles the tissue.

Furry
Friends

It's a Small-Pet World

Announcer: Hello, this is Ned Ratt reporting for MNN, the Mammal News Network. It's a big day here at the United Mammals, or UM. This is the first meeting of the Council for Small Mammal Pets. Our spokesmammal today is Ms. Ferrer of Peru, who represents the guinea pigs. Ms. Ferrer, thank you for the chance to learn more about small mammal pets.

Ms. Ferrer: Thank you, Mr. Ratt. We hope our meeting will help human beings become better friends to their small mammal pets. As a first step, we have written a Small Mammal Pet Bill of Rights. These are the rights of all small, fuzzy pets everywhere.

Announcer: Would you read them for us?

Ms. Ferrer: With pleasure. "We believe that each and every gerbil, hamster, mouse, guinea pig, and rabbit has the following rights:

1. To eat fresh, nutritious food every day

2. To be fed food free of harmful chemicals

3. To have fresh, clean water at all times

4. To live in a roomy cage in the shade

5. To have toys to play with that keep the mind and body active

6. To breathe fresh air

7. To be kept warm and free from drafts

8. To sleep on clean, fresh bedding

9. To enjoy the care and companionship of humans

10. To be left alone sometimes."

Pet Pointer

Never pick up a small animal by its ears or tail. Cup your hands around it or cuddle it loosely in your arms.

Announcer: We're sure those guidelines will be useful to all humans who keep small mammal pets. Now I'd like to ask a question of Mr. Hamster Haddad of Syria. Mr. Haddad, hamster owners have noticed that hamsters like to store away food in their cages. They also are able to carry lots of food in their cheek pouches. How do you explain this?

Mr. Haddad: Simple. My wild hamster relatives live in hot, dry areas of the world. They hunt for food at night, and sometimes they travel a long way to find it. So they collect as much as they can to eat when they need it. That's really very sensible.

Announcer: Mr. Gerbil Dorj of Mongolia, most of your relations also come from dry areas of the world. Are their habits just like a hamster's?

Mr. Dorj: Some wild gerbils store food. But we are different from hamsters in many ways. For example, we gerbils can live more easily in places where there is little water. We get the moisture we need from the food we eat. Another difference is that we are friendly animals. If we are not too crowded, we enjoy living together in family groups. Hamsters fight.

Announcer: What do you say to that, Mr. Haddad?

Mr. Haddad: I'm afraid it's true. We hamsters prefer not to live with other hamsters. But we're gentle with people when we get to know them, and we still make fine pets.

Announcer: Ms. Ferrer, we've heard from our friends from Syria and Mongolia. What can you tell us about your relatives?

Ms. Ferrer: Guinea pigs no longer live in the wild. All of them are *domesticated*. This means that people have been keeping my kind as pets for hundreds of years. Distant relatives of mine called *cavies* still live wild in South America, though.

Announcer: And now, we must end our telecast. Ms. Ferrer, do you have any closing remarks?

Ms. Ferrer: Yes. Thank you, Mr. Ratt and you viewers at home, for your interest in small mammal pets. Please remember that we are clean, friendly, gentle creatures. We ask only for a healthy living space and some company. In return, we pledge you our devotion and love.

Announcer: This has been Ned Ratt for MNN. Good night.

A Pet Word to Know

Mammal is the name for the large group of animals that have hair, a backbone, and a warm body temperature. Baby mammals get milk from their mother's body. Human beings, dogs, cats, hamsters, and rabbits are all mammals.

Hamsters Ham It Up

"Jamie! Joey! Come here!" Katie called. "Come see my hamster gym!" Her twin brothers hurried in. "See? I emptied out an old packing box from the basement. I left the top open and cut a door in the side. Then, just inside the door, I put a digging box filled with peat moss. Look at Goldie!" Katie exclaimed. Goldie, her favorite hamster, was burrowing as deep as she could.

Goldie's mother, Mandy, had raced through a toilet tissue roll to crawl across a stripped branch at the top. She was getting ready to slide down a paper towel roll.

Baby Angelina had raced ahead to the merry-go-round. She was running around and around on a wooden disk with a large bolt through the middle.

"I have so much fun at the gym," explained Katie, "that I decided to make a gym for our pets. Now they have a place to play besides their cages."

"What a great idea!" cried the twins.

Goldie, Mandy, and Angelina just kept playing. They seemed to think it was a good idea, too.

Pet Pointer

Wash foods before giving them to your hamster. Never let your pet hamster eat raw beans, potato buds, or the leafy greens from potatoes, carrots, or tomatoes. They are poisonous to hamsters.

Pet Project

A Taste of the Good Life, Hamster Style

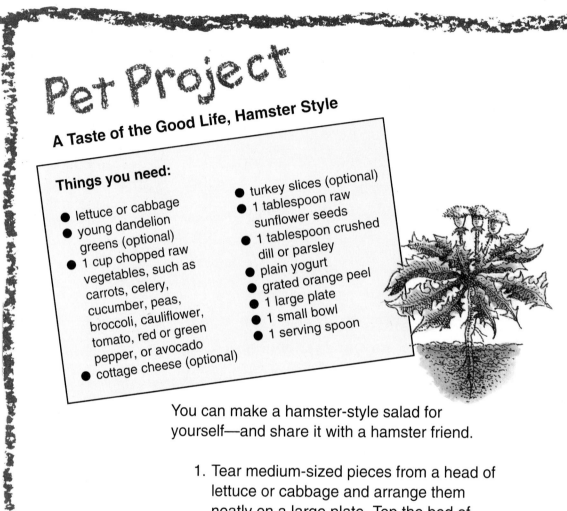

Things you need:

- lettuce or cabbage
- young dandelion greens (optional)
- 1 cup chopped raw vegetables, such as carrots, celery, cucumber, peas, broccoli, cauliflower, tomato, red or green pepper, or avocado
- cottage cheese (optional)
- turkey slices (optional)
- 1 tablespoon raw sunflower seeds
- 1 tablespoon crushed dill or parsley
- plain yogurt
- grated orange peel
- 1 large plate
- 1 small bowl
- 1 serving spoon

You can make a hamster-style salad for yourself—and share it with a hamster friend.

1. Tear medium-sized pieces from a head of lettuce or cabbage and arrange them neatly on a large plate. Top the bed of lettuce or cabbage with young dandelion greens if you have them.

2. Cover your bed of greens with the mixed raw vegetables.

3. Sprinkle sunflower seeds and crushed dill or parsley over the salad.

4. Put aside one tablespoon of the lettuce and mixed vegetables. If you wish, decorate the rest of your salad with turkey slices or cottage cheese.

5. Spoon a little yogurt into the small bowl. Add the grated orange peel to taste. Use this dressing to top your salad.

6. Eat the big salad all by yourself—and give your hamster the spoonful of vegetables you saved for a lunchtime treat.

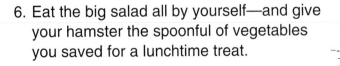

Adventures of a Second Grade Guinea Pig

When I first got here, I was scared to death! Why had I been snatched from my brothers and sisters? Where was I going? Who would take care of me? I trembled with fright.

Now, of course, I know I had nothing to fear. The cage in the pet shop was overcrowded. My brothers and I were beginning to fight, so the shop owner had found us all new homes. My brothers and sisters went to families. I was lucky—I was sent to a school.

My new cage smelled odd at first—or rather, it hardly smelled at all. I missed the scent of my old cage, but I was glad to have a clean, new one. And my new owner had mixed a few old wood shavings with the new ones in the cage. That made me feel right at home.

Before my owners brought me home, I lived in an old aquarium tank filled with thick wood chips. That home was nice, but I like this cage, too. Here, I have a wood frame box with walls of chicken wire. I like the way the wire mesh lets the fresh air in.

Of course, I've got everything here I need. The temperature is mild, and I have a little sunshine, but plenty of

It's a Pet Fact

No one knows for sure how guinea pigs got their name. But we do know some things: Guinea pigs grunt and squeal as pigs do. And they were first brought to England by traders. People in England bought the new pets for the price of— you guessed it— one guinea!

shade. My water bottle doesn't leak, and my bowl is always full of guinea pig pellets, hay, and carrot chunks to gnaw.

All the special attention I get makes me very happy. For example, I get to eat "people food" each day. The children feed me bits of corn and oats, and sometimes I even get orange slices or bread crusts soaked in milk.

The children take turns changing the bedding and petting me, so I get

care and company, but the teacher makes sure I'm not handled too much. And every afternoon, she watches me while I run free on the nature table.

Once, I even got to give the class a thrill. When the teacher looked away for a moment, I climbed all the way down to the floor! The children had a hard time trying to catch me—until I let them, of course. Why would I want to escape? I like it here!

Gerbils on the Move

What digs like a dog, burrows like a mole, scampers like a squirrel, and hops like a kangaroo? A gerbil! It's hard to guess how these quick little creatures will move. One second they're busy digging dirt with their front paws, and the next—where are they? Across the room? Underground?

Once a gerbil has left your hands or the cage, it might be almost anywhere. In fact, gerbils escape so easily that some western states have banned them! People there worry that gerbils will feel right at home in their warm, dry climate and become pests, like wild rats and mice.

It's lucky that most pet gerbils return to their own cages. If they didn't, we'd probably never see them once they escaped! Gerbils can "high jump"—often as high as their cages. And they tend to leap crazily in all directions.

They also scurry across rooms, between cracks, and into holes, only to emerge from an unexpected place! So hold your gerbil gently, but keep it snug—or you may be in for the chase of your life.

It's a Pet Fact

As smart as they are, most gerbils are terrible at making their way through a maze. They're so curious that they get sidetracked by other things. Then they forget to continue toward their goal.

Down at the Hutch

Greg read the sign aloud: "Welcome to the Rabbit Hutch."

"This is the place!" his sister Mary whispered excitedly. Their dad motioned her to ring the doorbell.

A smiling man with a handsome white mustache opened the door. "Well, hello there. I'll bet you're looking for a pet bunny. I'm Albert Turner. My wife, Ruby, and I raise rabbits at the Rabbit Hutch. Come on in, and let's talk."

Mary and Greg wanted to find out all about rabbits. But first they had to answer Mr. and Mrs. Turner's questions:

"Do you have a yard where a rabbit can hop around to get some exercise?"

"Is someone at home often enough? A rabbit needs attention."

"Will you care for the rabbit if it's sick and forgive it if it chews your baseball?"

Greg and Mary said yes to all those questions. "Those are very important questions," their father told Mr. and Mrs. Turner. "We're glad you asked."

"Well, then, let's meet the family," Mrs. Turner said.

A Pet Word to Know

Hutch is another word for a rabbit house or cage.

They went to the backyard, and Mr.
Turner began the introductions. "Ralph
and Alice and their babies live in this
hutch. We call these rabbits Mini Lops,"
he said.

Greg peered into the hutch. "Their
ears hang down!" he said.

"The ears on Lops are supposed to hang down," Mr. Turner told him. He lifted a baby by the skin at the back of its neck. He placed his other hand under the bunny's tail and held it firmly. "Hold a rabbit this way so it can't jump down and hurt itself," he explained.

Greg stroked the bunny gently. "That's right," Ruby said. "Always pet a rabbit in the direction its fur grows."

"Does their fur need brushing and washing, like our hair?" Mary asked.

"Yes and no," Mr. Turner answered. "You should brush rabbits, especially when they shed. But rabbits keep themselves clean. So you never need to bathe them."

"What kind of rabbits are those?" asked Mary, pointing to a set of rabbits in another hutch.

"Muffin and Cupcake and their bunnies are Angoras," Mrs. Turner answered. "Their fur is so soft and fine that people use it to make clothes. And those white ones are Florida whites. Don't they look like Easter bunnies?"

"What keeps their fur so soft?" Greg asked as he and Mary petted Muffin.

"The same thing that keeps all our rabbits healthy—rabbit pellets," Mr. Turner answered. He poured some tiny,

rod-shaped feed into Greg's hand. "These nuggets have every nutrient a rabbit needs."

"I thought rabbits ate carrots," Mary said with surprise as she let one of the Mini Lops sniff her hands.

"Well, a daily carrot is important," Mrs. Turner told her. "Rabbits' front teeth don't stop growing as people's teeth do. Chewing on carrots helps their teeth stay short."

Their father nodded at Mr. Turner, and Mr. Turner winked. "That baby Mini Lop seems to like you two. I think he's found himself a new family!"

Pet Pointer

Most of the year, a hutch should be kept outdoors in a shady place. In winter, you can keep a hutch in a well-lighted basement or garage.

Featured Creature

The little bunny squeezed
under the farmer's garden gate,
and lettuces and French beans
and radishes he ate.
The farmer saw him stealing
and chased him with his tools.
Bunny lost his bright blue jacket
and his little bunny shoes.
To save his life, he had to run
when the farmer turned his back.
Can you name the naughty bunny
who made such trouble for a snack?

ANSWER: Peter Rabbit

Birds
in the
Hand

A Canary Comes Home

Marcy, Alec, and Mrs. Johnson stood near Cary Canary's cage and looked out the apartment window. The cage was set back a bit from the window, away from drafts.

"What kind of birthday present do you think Dad will choose for C.C.?" asked Marcy.

"Maybe birdseed!" said Alec.

"We have plenty of that," Mrs. Johnson said. "I checked the bag when I filled the seed cup in his cage today."

"A nice new bath dish, then?" suggested Alec. It was Alec's job to bring C.C. his dish of bathwater every day. He enjoyed seeing C.C. splash in it. When C.C. was finished, Alec always removed

96

the bathing dish right away. It wasn't good for C.C. to drink the bathwater.

"Maybe Dad's getting C.C. new bells or a mirror to play with. Or a brand new cloth to cover his cage at night. Something pretty," cried Marcy, "with flowers!"

"No way," said Alec. "I bet he's getting him a new cuttlebone. C.C. loves to file his beak on that cuttlebone."

"Why do you suppose he likes his cuttlebone so much?" wondered Marcy.

"Because birds have fun chewing on things," said Mrs. Johnson. "And besides, when C.C. eats bits of the cuttlebone, he gets the calcium he needs to stay healthy."

"C.C. sure can make a mess in his cage. I'm glad Dad changes the paper at the bottom every day," Alec said.

Just then, C.C. sang out his lovely canary warble. "Whee-eet, whee-eet!" Mom, Marcy, and Alec wondered what the song was about.

"Maybe he's saying, 'Thank you for taking such good care of me,'" suggested Mrs. Johnson.

Just then, Marcy saw Mr. Johnson coming upstairs. "He's got two packages. And one of them is really big!" she shouted.

Dad put the two packages on the table. Alec ripped the paper off the big package. It was a shiny new bird cage, bigger than C.C.'s. And inside the small box was a tiny yellow bird.

"C.C. needs company when we're away all day," Dad announced. "Meet Mary Canary!"

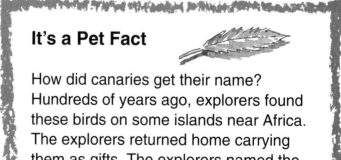

It's a Pet Fact

How did canaries get their name? Hundreds of years ago, explorers found these birds on some islands near Africa. The explorers returned home carrying them as gifts. The explorers named the birds after the place they found them— the Canary Islands.

They put the two birds in the new cage. C.C. sang out a sweet, happy melody.

"What a great present!" Marcy exclaimed. "And I think C.C. likes M.C., too. What do you think he's saying now?"

"I know!" said Alec. "C.C. just told us, 'Thanks for bringing home Mary Canary. She's even better than cuttlebone!'"

Who Wants Seconds?

When you're not hungry and eat only small portions, someone may say, "You're eating like a bird!" People think that because birds are small, they don't eat a lot. But birds have big appetites. In fact, some baby birds eat as much as their own weight in food every day!

Gardens, fields, and forests provide plenty of natural food for birds. But sometimes birds may have a hard time finding food. One reason is that in many areas, there is not as much open land as there once was. People have built homes, apartments, malls, or other buildings there. So there are fewer places to find seeds, insects, worms, and other foods that birds like.

Cold weather also makes it hard to find food. Many birds *migrate* in wintertime. This means they fly to warmer places. But birds that stay in cold winter places may not be able to get the food they usually eat. Insects are gone and seeds are often sealed under frozen ground or layers of snow.

But you can help the birds in your neighborhood. Bird feeders are a good way to do this.

Many things around your house make good bird feeders. A plastic milk or soda bottle or other sturdy container works well. Ask a grown-up to help you cut holes in it and fill it with bird food. Then hang it on a tree, fence, or wall.

Have you ever seen a bird feeder set at the top of a pole with a metal dish or cone under it? That's done to keep squirrels and larger animals away from the birds' food. It also protects birds from attack by cats or other animals while they are eating.

Perhaps you live where there's no yard or trees to hold a feeder. That's okay. You can still feed birds in other ways. A clothes hanger makes a feeder that you can hang on a window sill. First, thread popcorn, cranberries, apple slices, or dried fruit on strings. Wrap the strings around the hanger or tie them so they hang down.

Birds also like *suet,* a special kind of animal fat you can get from a butcher. Ask a grown-up to cut the suet into chunks and help you attach it to a tree or a fence. You can also put suet in a mesh bag, the kind that holds potatoes or onions from the market. Hang the bag of suet on a branch or outside a window, and your birds will have a hearty treat!

Find out about other food for birds. You can buy birdseed in pet shops, hardware stores, and grocery stores. Birds also like chopped dog biscuits, breadcrumbs, and nuts. Ears of corn make good bird food, too.

However you help the birds in your neighborhood, you can be certain that they will appreciate it. In fact, if you watch quietly, you will surely see birds come back for second helpings.

Pet Pointer

When you start feeding wild birds, especially in winter, always stick with it. When food is scarce, birds return again and again to the same supply. They might even stop looking elsewhere. If food isn't where they expect to find it, they may starve.

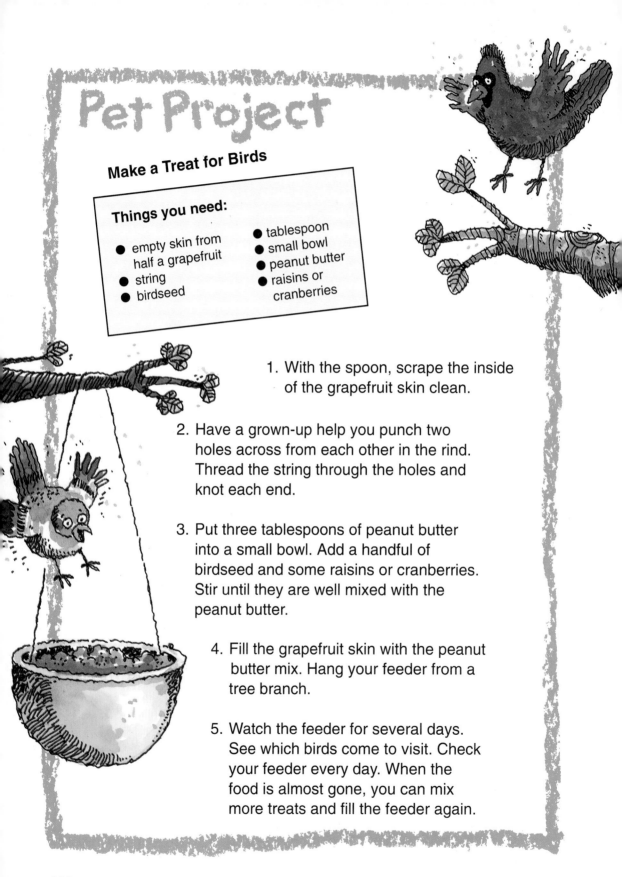

Pet Project

Make a Treat for Birds

Things you need:

- empty skin from half a grapefruit
- string
- birdseed
- tablespoon
- small bowl
- peanut butter
- raisins or cranberries

1. With the spoon, scrape the inside of the grapefruit skin clean.

2. Have a grown-up help you punch two holes across from each other in the rind. Thread the string through the holes and knot each end.

3. Put three tablespoons of peanut butter into a small bowl. Add a handful of birdseed and some raisins or cranberries. Stir until they are well mixed with the peanut butter.

4. Fill the grapefruit skin with the peanut butter mix. Hang your feeder from a tree branch.

5. Watch the feeder for several days. See which birds come to visit. Check your feeder every day. When the food is almost gone, you can mix more treats and fill the feeder again.

The Keet Report

Hello out there in TV land! Welcome to The Keet Report. I'm your host, Perry Keet. Tonight, we have a very special show. It's about talking, a skill shared by a few talented birds.

Let's welcome our panel. Myna Byrd is a myna. I understand you flew in from Asia to be with us. Thank you. Hercule Parrot is an African gray, all the way from Kenya. And Corky Tiel is the head cockatiel at Zimmy's Pet Store.

So, folks, you're all talkers?

Myna: Yes and no, Perry. Let's make sure our viewers understand that birds can't really talk the way people do.

Corky: That's right. We talking birds are just good at *mimicking,* or imitating sounds we hear. As pets, we can learn lots of sounds and words. And scientists are finding that we may even understand simple ideas like "yes" and "no" and "same" and "different." But we still can't carry on a conversation.

Perry: I have heard that even though tame parrots are excellent mimics, wild parrots don't mimic at all.

Hercule: Wild parrots imitate the screams and squawks of their parents, but not the sounds of other animals.

Perry: Then why do caged parrots mimic people's speech?

Hercule: People think that a young parrot may learn to mimic human sounds if it thinks of its owners as its parents or part of its flock. Also, we parrots are very intelligent animals. In a cage, we're by ourselves. We can't fly around and do the things our wild relatives do, and we get bored. So we start to imitate the sounds we hear just for fun.

Perry: And it is fun, isn't it? Now let's talk a bit about our beaks. Are ours somehow different from other birds' beaks? Is that how we're able to talk?

Corky: No. We make sounds by using the lower part of our windpipes.

Myna: But no one knows exactly why we can mimic but other birds can't.

Perry: How did you learn your skills, Hercule?

Hercule: It takes many months. My owner had lots of patience. First she trained me to do tricks, such as perch on her hand.

Corky: My owner, Mr. Zimmerman, taught me how to pay attention to his voice. He gave me lessons in his office, away from other birds and loud noises.

Myna: My owners spoke slowly and clearly, saying a word over and over until I repeated it.

Hercule: After I learned single words, it was easy to say phrases. I was even taught to recite a poem!

Corky: I think we should tell our audience that some birds never learn to talk, even though their owners do everything right.

Perry: Well folks, our time is up. We hope you've enjoyed tonight's show. Tune in next week for a special feature, "Cuttlebone, is it a snack or a toy?" Good night.

Duck Walk

"Roll out the red carpet and start the music. Here they come!" The marchers proudly make their way down a red carpet. Nearby, a cheering crowd snaps photographs.

Who are these famous people? Are they princes and princesses? No, they're not royalty. In fact, they're not people at all. They're ducks! And they aren't parading through a royal palace. These lucky ducks are marching through the lobby of the Peabody Hotel in Memphis, Tennessee.

One day way back in the 1930's, the manager of the Peabody brought some ducks to the hotel. He thought that the guests would enjoy watching them swim in the fountain. He was right! Ducks have been entertaining guests at the Peabody Hotel ever since.

And the ducks have a lot more space to knock around in today. At night, they live on the hotel's roof, known as the "Royal Duck Palace." The whole palace is carpeted to protect the ducks' webbed feet! They even have their own bathing pool to swim in. At night, they sleep in the "Royal Bed Chamber," a beautiful tent made of curtains and topped with a crown.

A little before eleven o'clock every morning, the ducks waddle out of their rooftop home. Their trainer leads them to an express elevator. They pile in and ride down to the main floor lobby. Now the fun begins.

A bouncy marching tune blares forth from a tape recorder. All eyes are on the elevator door. Imagine the excitement in the air!

Somebody calls out, "Here come the ducks!"

Tap-tap-tap. The trainer's cane guides the performers. One by one, they take their place in line. A mallard drake, the only male, leads the way, and four hens bring up the rear. In perfect duck formation, they waddle to a beautiful marble fountain. When they get there, they jump right in.

All day long, they swim, dive, and splash. People watch and take pictures.

At five o'clock, it's time for the ducks to march back to the elevator. Up they go, back to their rooftop tent. A meal fit for kings is probably waiting for them.

How long will this good life last? Sorry, prince and princesses, only a few months. After that, back to the farm you go. There, your pool will be a pond, and your only audience will be the other farm animals. At the hotel, another group of ducks takes your place.

Do you think the lucky ducks will miss their good life at the hotel? Maybe every night in their sweet duck dreams, they'll waddle out of the Royal Duck Palace and splash in the marble fountain of the Peabody Hotel.

Old Mr. Periwinkle

Time to wake up? Well, let me stretch my wings and fluff my feathers, and then I'll tell you about my life with the Gibson family. It was 1940 when I joined them. Walter's Aunt Mabel brought me as a gift when Walter and Audrey got married. I'm more than fifty years old.

I got plenty of attention the first year. Walter was busy at his job, and Audrey was learning to cook. But they found time for my talking lessons. Pretty soon, I could say whole sentences.

All that attention ended when Wally Junior was born. At first I was jealous. After all, I was a young parrot. I was used to getting lots of attention. When I felt ignored, I'd throw peanut shells on the floor and spill my water dish. Pretty soon, Walter and Audrey figured out what was wrong. They started bringing my perch into the kitchen at mealtimes. They talked to me and gave me special treats, like table scraps. Yum.

Wally, Jr., arrives. Now we have 2 "kids"!

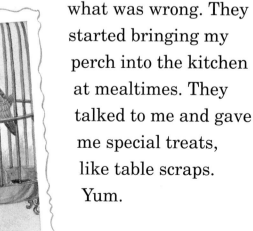

I behaved better, and everyone was happier. I got used to staying in my cage while the baby was around. Because I was so good, Audrey always took me out of the cage while he was napping. And after a while I got to like little Wally.

Before we knew it, Wally was saying *his* first words, "Mama, more." Too bad Walter wasn't there to hear them, but he was away at a big war. Audrey showed Wally his dad's photo every day, until the happy day Walter returned home.

An apple a day is good for Wally— and Mr. P.

Wally grew like a weed. I didn't have much to do with him when he was small. But when he got bigger, he became a good friend. I liked to climb on his shoulders and tug on his hair with my beak. He had such curly hair! "That tickles, Mr. P.," he'd say. "That tickles, Mr. P.," I'd say back. Every day, he brought me a piece of juicy, red apple to eat.

Christmas, 1953.
Mr. P. is a big help
with decorating!

When Wally was eight, baby Sarah came along. She was cute, cooing and smiling. She had no hair at all.

The holiday season was always my favorite time of year. All the good things to eat, pretty sparkling lights to look at, and shiny paper to play with! Best of all, though, was decorating the tree. Every year, Sarah got to put a little green glass parrot on one of the limbs. "Look," they said, "it's Mr. Periwinkle in the tree!" I was so proud.

Well, time flies. Before we knew it, Sarah was in school. Then in no time at

all, Wally was graduating. I missed him
so much when he went off to college. But
Sarah gave me my apples then.

One day, Wally brought home a bride.
They posed for a photograph right next to
my cage. Now the picture sits on the
coffee table. I look at it every day.

Sarah joined the Peace Corps and
went to South America. She sent me a
picture post card with birds on it and
wrote, "These are cousins from the
Periwinkle side of the family." Then she
got married, too.

Now that the children are on their own, the three of us lead a quiet life. Audrey and Walter have retired from their jobs, but they keep busy with hobbies. Sometimes at night Walter puts a record on and they dance. I sit on my perch and sway in time to the music. Then they take me out and I sit on Walter's arm while we read or watch TV. Walter doesn't have much hair to tug on. So now I nibble his sweater.

Sarah and her husband come over often with their twins. Too bad the little fellows can't say "Mr. Periwinkle" yet. They say "Miss Poowink." Everyone laughs when I imitate them.

I think I have the nicest family in the world. Just the other day, I heard Sarah talking to the twins. She said that when they get big enough, they can feed me a piece of apple. I can hardly wait!

The Courtship of Tony and Cleo

Tony the cockatiel perched in his cage at Sam's Pet Shop. Customers came and went all day long. But Tony hardly noticed. His round black eyes were always on the girl cockatiel in the next aisle. He knew she was beautiful. But that's all he knew about her. "If only we could meet," he sighed.

In the cage across the aisle sat a girl cockatiel named Cleo. She had soft, gray feathers and a little gray crest. She took shy looks at the handsome boy cockatiel named Tony. She thought it was cute when he drummed on his perch with his beak or whistled a melody at her when he knew she was paying attention.

One day, a couple walked in with their daughter. "Here's a nice cockatiel!" the girl exclaimed, pointing to Tony. "I like his bright orange cheeks and his yellow crest."

Tony listened as Sam told the family how friendly and affectionate cockatiels were. "It would be nice to go home with them," Tony thought, "but how I would miss Cleo!"

A Pet Word to Know

An **aviary** is a large cage for birds. An aviary can be indoors or outside. An aviary is a good place for birds to live. They have more space to fly around than in a smaller cage. Some people build their own aviaries, often attached to a building.

Cleo was listening, too. What would she do if Tony went away? She'd be so lonely. "Peeeep!" she cried.

The family turned to see where the noise was coming from. "Oh, what kind of bird is that?" the daughter asked. "It looks like Tony, except not as colorful."

"That's a female cockatiel," Sam replied. "Why not buy the pair? Cockatiels like to live together."

"That's exactly what we've been planning," said the mother.

Tony and Cleo could hardly believe what they were hearing. Maybe their wishes would come true!

Sure enough, within the hour the cockatiels had arrived at their new home.

Their comfortable cage had lots of perches and plenty of room for flying around. Then the couple saw something special in the corner—a nesting box. It

was a little bigger than a shoebox, with a
perch under the entrance hole. Both Tony
and Cleo were delighted. Tony made
happy sounds, "Whee—whee!"

On the days that followed, Tony often
whistled to Cleo and scratched the
feathers on her head. Cleo didn't show it,
but she was pleased with the attention.

The pair entered their nesting box to
prepare for a family. Cleo soon laid five
small, white eggs. In the days that
followed, Tony sat on the eggs during the
day, and Cleo took over at night.

Almost three weeks later, five downy yellow chicks hatched. Tony and Cleo fed them and sheltered them under their wings. In about a week, the chicks' gray feathers had started to grow. And three weeks after that, they poked their heads out of the nesting box for the first time.

Raising five hungry chicks was a lot of work. But Tony and Cleo were proud of their family. They knew that they would soon start another.

Featured Creature

A mother waited patiently
for her little ones to hatch.
One by one, they all came out,
but the last one didn't match.
"He's so big and gray and clumsy,"
all the other birds would say.
They pecked and poked and laughed at him,
'til he finally ran away.
But through the winter something changed,
and when the ice was gone,
his reflection in the still, dark lake
showed that he'd become a swan.
Who is he?

Answer: the Ugly Duckling

Sir Terrence's Tour

Pay attention, everyone. You say you want a real adventure? Well, you've come to the right place. I'm Sir Terrence MacTurtle. Like all the MacTurtles before me, I take brave and curious young people on safaris into the wild. There, we come face to face with the wondrous creatures that live in ponds, on lily pads, and in the damp, dark spaces under fallen logs.

So climb in my All-Terrain Turtlemobile, and let's see what we find!

Shh. . . . Here's our first sighting. Point your binoculars over there, toward the shallow water near the pond's edge. See that big shiny green creature? She's a bullfrog. Does anyone know what group of animals she belongs to? Did I hear someone say "amphibian"? That's right. Notice how smooth and moist her skin is. She and her amphibian cousins need to stay near water all the time. That's where they lay their eggs.

Now we'll pull over to the sunny side of the pond. Hold on tight! It could be a bumpy ride.

Ahhh, here we are. Look at those lazy chaps, sunning on the rocks. They're my relatives. We haven't much in common, though, except that we're all turtles.

Turtles are reptiles. What makes a reptile a reptile, you ask? Take a look at my skin. Don't be afraid to touch. It feels leathery and scaly, doesn't it? That's not from too much sun! All reptiles have skin like this. Most reptiles live on land, and that's where we lay our eggs. But some, like me, also spend time in water. Lizards and snakes are reptiles, too.

What's that? Look there. See that handsome green fellow paddling through the water with his long, flat tail? He's a newt. He may be shaped like a lizard, but he's an amphibian. Look at those red spots. He's a beauty, to be sure. Bet he's out looking for a juicy fly or a tasty worm to snack on.

Climb back into the ATT, and we'll drive into the woods. Oh ho! What luck! Look at that fat fellow crossing the road. Can you see his bumpy, brown skin? Does anyone know what he is? Right! He's a toad, another type of amphibian. But unlike frogs, toads have dry skin. They don't need to be close to water all the time—only when it's time to lay eggs. And no, you can't get warts from touching a toad. Who told you that nonsense?

Remember the handsome newt we saw earlier? If we're very quiet and patient in the dim woods, we may meet one of his land-dwelling relatives scuffling about in the dead leaves. Wait, there's one now. Notice the dark skin and the bright yellow markings. He's a spotted salamander. Oh dear, he's heard us. Off he goes, under a log. He and his kind are quite shy.

That's the end of our tour. You've had a chance to see some of these delightful animals in the wild. If you ever decide to keep one as a pet, you should try to give it a home that matches its natural environment. Now you have a head start in knowing how to create that home!

Featured Creature

A certain hare is fleet of foot,
But speed is what I lack.
You'd find it hard to run, I'm sure,
With your house upon your back.
So when the hare announced, "Let's race!"
It seemed to all I'd lose.
But midway through, my long-eared friend
Stopped to take a snooze.

I, meanwhile, plodded slowly on.
I never did give in.
At last, I passed the sleeping hare
And trudged bravely on to win!
When the hare woke up, he knew he'd lost.
He wore a shameful face.
But of me, that wise old Aesop said,
"Slow and steady wins the race."
Who am I?

ANSWER: the tortoise

Turtle Talk

Where do turtles live?

They live in all kinds of places. Some swim in the ocean. Others roam about in woods and meadows. Turtles live in ponds, streams, lakes, and even in deserts.

What is a turtle's shell made of?

Most turtles have two-layer shells. The inner layer is made of bone and is attached to the turtle's skeleton. The outer layer, which is tough and hard, is made of dead skin cells. The turtle replaces these cells in much the same way that you grow hair.

It's a Pet Fact

Turtles are the only reptiles that have shells.

Where should I keep a turtle?

Most small turtles do well in a terrarium. The amount of water in the terrarium depends on the type of turtle you have. A few kinds need lots of water to swim in as well as to drink. Desert tortoises never swim and can go for a long time without drinking. Turtles also need a warm, dry, well-lit place to rest and bask.

How can I tell if a turtle is healthy?

A turtle's eyes should be open and alert. If you pick the turtle up, it should pull its head, arms, and legs into its shell, or it should make strong swimming motions. Never buy a turtle with puffy eyes or a soft shell.

Do turtles live a long time?

Yes, indeed. Some Galapagos tortoises and box turtles live for more than one hundred years!

Pet Word to Know

Tortoise is another name for a turtle that lives on land.

At the Salamanders'

Well, hello, darlings. I'm Samantha Salamander, and this is my home. Lovely, isn't it? I want you to know that the world's most famous terrarium designer created this perfect living space for my husband, Salvador, and me.

Salvador and I are red salamanders. We come from the woods of the eastern United States. Here in our gracious home we have everything we would have in our natural environment—water to swim in, food to eat, fresh air. Where is Salvador, anyway? He should come out and greet his guests!

For a short time, we salamanders can live quite comfortably in a large jar. But a spacious terrarium like ours is much nicer. All salamanders like moist air. See the ceiling? It's glass to keep in moisture, with an opening to let air in. Other salamander homes have a lid of wire screen. Some are partly covered with plastic wrap to keep the moisture in.

Look at this magnificent piece of wood. Salvador and I sometimes rest on it most of the day. But my favorite piece of furniture is this exquisite rock. Look at

how cool and dark it is underneath. It's a
wonderful hiding place for a salamander!
And these leaves and soil are absolutely
delightful to crawl around in.

Come, darlings, and I'll show you the
pool. It's a nice ceramic dish buried in the
soil at the bottom of the terrarium. My
husband and I need water, but we swim
only sometimes. Other salamander
friends of ours, especially some of the
newts, like to spend all their time in the

water. Their homes are made almost entirely of water. Imagine!

Oh, there's Salvador, hiding behind that fern. He's always hiding. Sal, dear, come out and greet our guests. Sal? Sal! He never listens.

All these plants give Salvador so many places to hide. They also produce oxygen for Salvador and me to breathe. I think they make our terrarium more attractive, don't you?

Well, it looks as though Salvador won't come out today. I suppose a salamander has a right to his privacy. But maybe he'll be less shy next time you visit.

Presto Change-O: A Tadpole Turns into a Frog

If you keep an eye on frogs, you will see one of the most wonderful magic acts in nature. It begins after a female frog lays her eggs, usually in the spring. In time, the eggs hatch into tiny babies called *tadpoles*.

A newborn tadpole looks more like a fish than a frog. It has a long tail and a bulgy, round head, and it spends all its

bullfrog tadpole

time in the water. Like a fish, the tadpole has no lungs for breathing air. It uses special organs called *gills* to take oxygen from the water.

As the tadpole grows, something amazing happens. Hind legs, and then front legs, sprout from the tadpole's sides. Meanwhile, the tadpole's tail starts shrinking. Soon, the lungs finish their development, and the gills disappear. Now the tadpole likes to crawl out of the water and rest on a rock or a piece of driftwood. In time, anywhere from weeks to years, the tadpole turns into a frog.

If you live near a river, lake, or pond, you can raise your own tadpoles. Have a grownup take you to the water in the spring and help you find a clump of eggs. Collect a few (be sure not to take them all) and put them in a tank filled with pond water. Soon, the eggs will hatch into tadpoles.

It's a Pet Fact

It takes three years for a bullfrog tadpole to turn into an adult bullfrog.

A small tank will hold about six tadpoles. Feed the tadpoles water plants or boiled lettuce or spinach. High-protein dry baby cereal is also good tadpole food. When the water level in the tank drops, add fresh pond water. Some tap water contains chlorine, which is harmful to fish and tadpoles. If you must use tap water, fill a large jar and let the water sit for a few days to get rid of the chlorine.

As their legs and lungs develop, the tadpoles will need to climb out of the water to rest and breathe. So put a rock or a piece of wood in the tank. After the tadpoles turn into frogs, release them where you found the eggs.

If you want to keep one or two frogs as pets, put them in a moist terrarium with a dish of water. Feed them a varied diet. Many kinds of frogs like crickets and other insects or earthworms.

Remember that frogs will eat only food that is moving. If you can't get live food for your frog, you have to pretend it's alive. Take a bit of lean meat and tie it to a long piece of string. Then, dangle it in front of the frog, jiggling it slightly. The hungry frog will do just what it does in the wild—stick out its long tongue and gobble up the food. You can do this several times until the frog seems to be satisfied.

Pet Word to Know

Metamorphosis (*meht uh MAWR fuh sihs*) is the word we use for the process by which an animal changes its form, such as a tadpole turning into a frog.

A Wonderful, Watery World

When you look into an aquarium, you are looking into a colorful, exciting world. Many people find that watching the smooth, graceful movement of the fish is peaceful and relaxing. Keeping fish as pets is fun. But before you decide to start an aquarium, you have some decisions to make.

Many people with aquariums keep tropical fish, since they are so colorful and come in so many shapes and sizes. In general, the easiest fish to care for are freshwater fish.

At a pet store, you can buy the supplies you need to set up an aquarium and books that tell how to do it. Many people choose a ten- or twenty-gallon (38- or 76-liter) tank. Cover the bottom of the tank with medium-sized gravel. Then place live or plastic aquarium plants here and there to make your tank beautiful. Putting in a few rocks adds variety to the scene and gives your fish a place to hide.

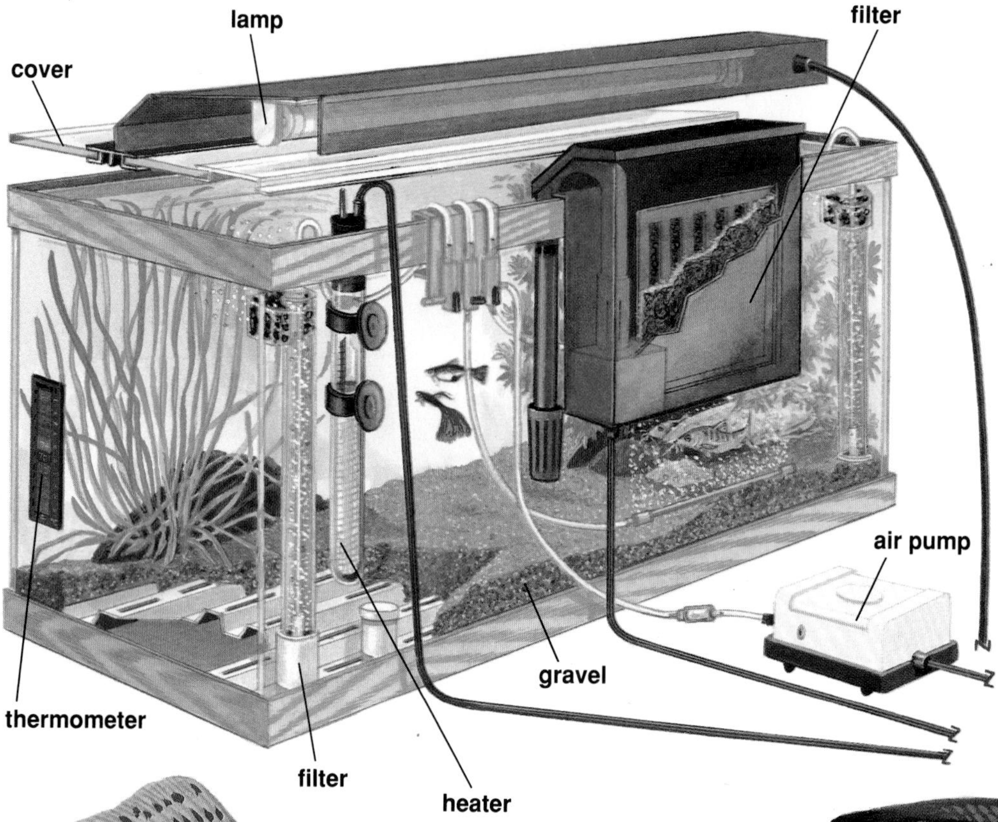

Labels on illustration:
cover · lamp · filter · thermometer · filter · heater · gravel · air pump

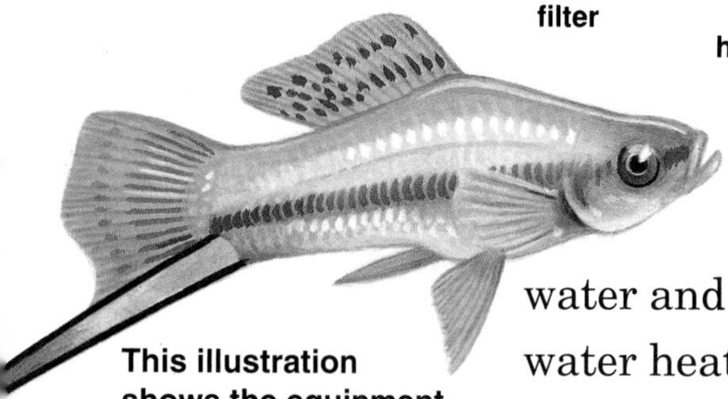

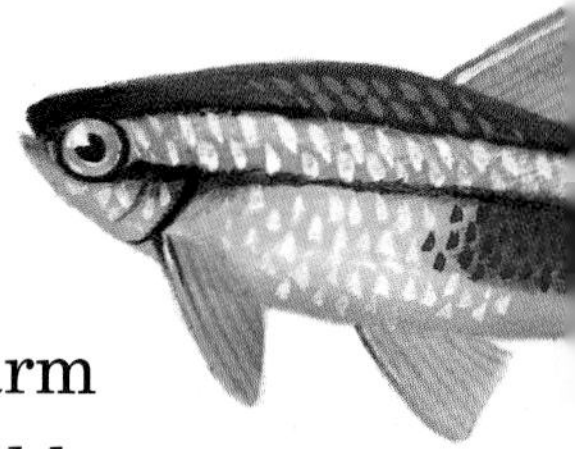

This illustration shows the equipment you need to make an aquarium a healthy place for fish to live. An air pump and filter keep the water clean. The filter can hang outside the tank or be buried under the gravel. A heater and thermometer help you control the water temperature. A cover keeps the heat—and the fish—in the tank.

Tropical fish need warm water and light. Your tank should have a water heater and a thermometer to keep the water at the proper temperature. A fluorescent light with a timer, mounted in the hood of the aquarium, can help you control the amount of light your tank receives. Experiment to find out how much light your tank needs.

And of course, it's very important to keep the water clean. A water filter and pump take care of that. An air pump also helps keep the water fresh.

Pet stores sell prepared foods that provide excellent nourishment for your fish. It's also good to feed the fish live food sometimes. Tubifex worms and brine shrimp are some favorite foods of tropical fish. Feed your fish every day, but never overfeed them. Uneaten food sinks to the bottom of the tank and decays. Decaying produces bacteria that can harm or even kill the fish.

Your aquarium may need cleaning as often as every week or two. Drain one-fourth to one-third of the water in the tank, using a siphon hose. You also can use the hose to vacuum up dirt from the gravel floor. Use a scraper to remove algae from the walls, and wipe the part of the glass above the water with a damp sponge. Never use soap, because it will poison the fish. After cleaning, refill the tank using tap water that you have *dechlorinated* by letting it sit in an uncovered container for a few days.

With proper care, your fish should provide many hours of enjoyment. It's fun to imagine what it would be like to be a fish, living in that watery world.

Pet Pointer

Little South American fish called *guppies* are a good choice to start your new aquarium. Guppies don't fight, and they don't get sick very often. It's fun to watch them swim around the tank, especially the pretty rainbow-colored males.

Dear Mrs. Nugget

PET NEWS

DEAR MRS. NUGGET

Dear Mrs. Nugget,
My darling swordtail has been acting funny! It stays near the top of the water, and it holds its fins close to its side. Could it be sick?
Signed,
Worried

Dear Worried,
Yes. It may be having trouble breathing because tiny animals called *parasites* have attacked its gills. Put your swordtail in a separate tank so the parasites won't spread to your other fish. Then ask your pet store for medication. While we're on the subject, it's important to control the water temperature, feed your fish a good diet, and keep an eye on them for signs of other illnesses. For example, white spots on the skin mean your fish have a disease called *ich*. Pet stores sell drops to put in the water to cure ich.

Dear Mrs. Nugget,
I bought a beautiful new angelfish last week to keep my other angelfish company. But when I put it in the tank, the other one attacked it. Why?
Signed,
Caught in the Middle

Dear Caught,
Angelfish are *territorial*. This means that they don't like to share their space with other fish. The best thing to do is to keep the fish apart for a few days. Put one of them in a type of cage called a *net breeder* inside the aquarium or in a separate tank. When the angelfish get used to each other, they may make peace. Good luck.

Dear Mrs. Nugget,
My tank always seems messy, even though I clean it every week. Bits of food collect in the gravel, and a green film grows on the glass. How can I keep it clean between washings?
Signed,
Need a Maid

Dear Need a Maid,
Certain types of fish can help you keep your tank clean. Catfish called *corydoras* are especially hardworking "maids." They clean the gravel at the bottom of the tank. And the green film that bothers you is algae. A water snail or a little fish called an *algae eater* will gobble algae right up!

When Is a Horse Not a Horse?

What has the head of a horse, the tail of a monkey, and the fins and gills of a fish? What is really a dad but acts like a mom? It's a fish called a *sea horse,* one of the world's strangest creatures!

You may find a sea horse in a home aquarium, its long tail wrapped around a plant or a piece of coral. There, it waits for tiny creatures to swim by, then sucks them into its tubelike mouth. Then you may see the sea horse gracefully uncoil its tail from its anchor and swim away, "standing" straight up! It powers itself mostly with the single fin on its back.

Perhaps the most unusual thing about sea horses is the fact that the father—not the mother—"gives birth" to the young. How can this be? During mating, one or more females deposit eggs into a special pouch on the male's belly. The tiny babies emerge from Dad's pouch from a few days to a few weeks later.

Most adult sea horses are less than six inches (15 centimeters) long. The largest sea horses grow to about twelve inches (30 centimeters). But sorry, they're still too small to ride!

Seahorse Family Growth Chart

The Monterey Bay Aquarium on the California coast exhibits plants and animals that live in Monterey Bay. The Kelp Forest exhibit, *above*, features animals that live among giant strands of *kelp*, a type of seaweed.

The Big Tanks

You've seen that it takes work to keep wet pets happy and healthy at home or at school. So can you imagine what a big job it is to run a public aquarium? There, huge tanks display many kinds of fish, including sharks, rays, and eels, and such other sea creatures as coral and anemones. Many aquariums have seals, dolphins, and other sea mammals as well. Some even have special "touch pools" where visitors can handle small sea creatures.

It takes lots of people and equipment to keep a public aquarium running—scientists, business managers, educators, and technicians. All of these people work to make the aquarium a place where you can discover the magical world beneath the water.

At the Monterey Bay Aquarium's touch pool, *below*, visitors can touch sea creatures that are safe to handle, such as crabs, rays, and starfish.

At Chicago's John G. Shedd Aquarium, *right,* creatures in the Coral Reef exhibit get a daily feeding. Here a diver feeds a shark while talking to the audience through a special microphone. Other people work behind the scenes to keep an aquarium running smoothly. At the Aquarium of the Americas in New Orleans, Louisiana, *below,* a technician mixes vitamin powder to add to the tanks. This makes the tank water more like real seawater.

Veterinarians care for the animals that live in aquariums and for injured wild sea animals, as well. These veterinarians at Sea World in San Diego, California, are treating a California sea lion. When it is well, they will return it to the wild.

Aquariums try to re-create the natural habitats of the sea creatures that live there. For tropical fish like these, aquarium designers added plants, coral, and rocks. Having a home like their natural one is healthier for the animals, and it helps visitors learn more about undersea life.

Farmyard Friends

The Horse
and Pony Show

Pssst! Hello, friend. My name is Moonlight Bright. I'm new here—this is my first major horse show!

So far, it's all been pretty exciting. Last Friday, the blacksmith and farrier came to trim my hoofs and make new shoes. On Monday, my owner, Carly, came into my stall wearing brand new boots.

After she tacked me and led me out of the barn, Carly told me what to expect at the show. She said I'd see hundreds of horses and ponies. Some of them would even be Tennessee walkers, like me!

Carly said we'll compete for ribbons and points. The horse with the most points in its *division*, or part of the show, will be declared the winner. And, friend,

Pet Words to Know

Farrier is the name for a person who fits a horse with horseshoes.

To **tack** a horse is to put on its bridle and saddle or harness.

I really don't mean to brag, but I think we can win this show!

My partner has groomed me well, so I'm sure to make a good impression. This morning, she massaged me with the curry comb to loosen any dirt and dead hair. Then she brushed me with a hard brush to get my coat clean. Next she fixed my tail so it looks like a waterfall!

Carly washed me, head to hoof, with sweet-smelling baby shampoo. Then she rinsed me with a hose and a sponge and scraped the water from my coat. Finally, she rubbed my coat to make it shine. For a finishing touch, she oiled my hoofs.

Of course, this show is more than a beauty contest. As a Tennessee walker, Carly says, I'll be judged for my walk,

running walk, and canter. I can't wait to show my running walk—just fast enough to satisfy the show rules, but slow enough for a smooth, easy ride.

So I'm shining clean, trained, and ready to go. Do I look okay to you? You can tell I'm excited, but I'm not at all tense. I just hope I stay calm when they call my name. Wish me luck!

It's a Pet Fact

The smooth gait of the Tennessee walking horse has earned it the nickname of "nature's rocking chair."

Giddyup!

It's a Pet Fact

Horse shows have many kinds of competitions. English riders compete in a number of divisions, such as *equitation* (horsemanship), hunting, and jumping. The Western division has some special competitions, including *stock*, to judge steady speed and control; *pleasure horse*, to judge a horse's gaits; and *trail*, with obstacles and ditches.

Tracy and Jack got out of the truck and walked over to the barn. "Hi, Mr. Mackey," called Tracy. "I brought Jack for his first riding lesson!"

"Glad to meet you, Jack," said Mr. Mackey. "This is Sophie, my Morgan horse.

"We'll approach Sophie from the front and a bit to the side, so we don't spook her," said Mr. Mackey. "And you'll mount on the left."

"She's so big!" exclaimed Jack. "How do I get on?"

"Just put your left foot in the stirrup, grab the saddle, lift yourself up, and swing your right leg over! It's a big step," laughed Tracy, "but you can make it."

Mr. Mackey watched Jack mount the horse. "Now, sit up straight, with your back and shoulders relaxed. Keep your heels down.

"Take the reins lightly in your left hand. You'll need them to control the horse. But take care not to pull on them, except to hold back a little when you stop. Pulling the reins can hurt the horse's mouth."

"We do Western riding," added Tracy. "In English riding, you pull the reins to turn the horse's head in the direction you want to go. But in Western riding, you just set the reins on the horse's neck. The touch of the reins on one side will make the horse turn to the other."

"But how do I get her going?" asked Jack.

Mr. Mackey smiled. "Just press your legs together gently."

Jack did it, and Sophie began to walk! "Hey!" he cried. "I'm riding! I'm at the races!"

"Whoa!" laughed Mr. Mackey. "You've only learned to walk. You've still got to learn to trot, canter, and gallop. Not to mention the fact that you haven't tried stopping."

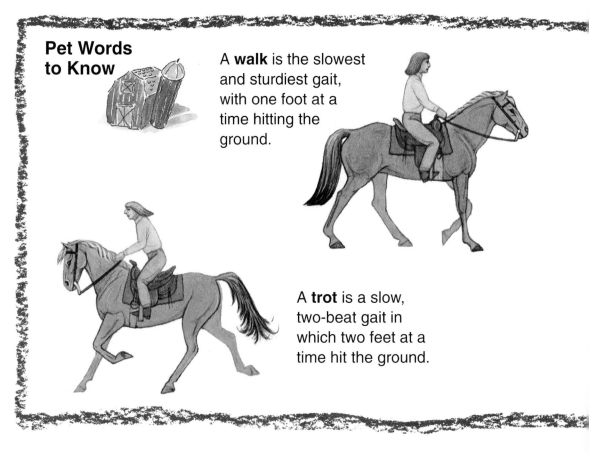

Pet Words to Know

A **walk** is the slowest and sturdiest gait, with one foot at a time hitting the ground.

A **trot** is a slow, two-beat gait in which two feet at a time hit the ground.

"Oh, yeah," grinned Jack. "Hold back a little on the reins—"

"Gently," warned Tracy. Jack tried it, and stopped!

"Mr. Mackey," he said. "This is great! I want to learn it all: trotting, cantering, and galloping, and handling obstacles, too. Then maybe I can go trail riding, like Tracy. Will you work with me?"

Mr. Mackey smiled at Jack. "Let's go and groom Sophie, and we'll set up your schedule," he said.

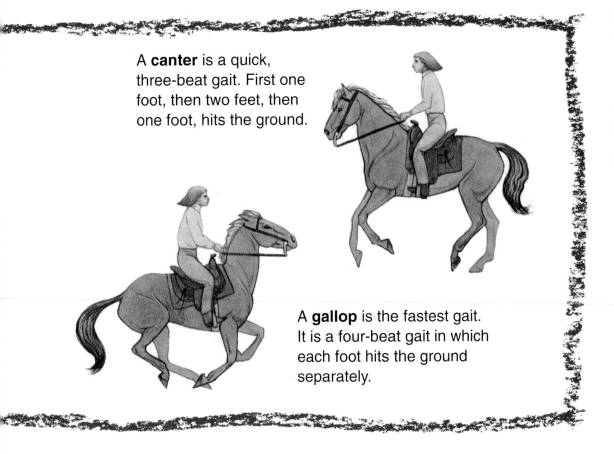

A **canter** is a quick, three-beat gait. First one foot, then two feet, then one foot, hits the ground.

A **gallop** is the fastest gait. It is a four-beat gait in which each foot hits the ground separately.

Going Whole Hog

"This room is a pigsty!" your father says, and you promise to clean it up—some time soon. But if you visit a pig, you might notice that a pigsty is not such a bad place to live. In fact, the pig's pen might be cleaner than your own bedroom!

No one knows for sure why pigs have such a bad name. However, they have been slandered for thousands of years. Actually, pigs are smart, clean, curious, and social.

Smart pigs have been trained to hunt small game and sniff out *truffles*, the delicious, hard-to-find mushrooms that grow underground. They probably find as many truffles in a day as a dog could find in a week.

Pigs also have been taught to pull small carts and jump through circus hoops. Long ago, King Louis XI of France had pigs trained to cheer him up—he liked to watch them dance!

It's hard to believe, but pigs prefer to be clean. They will sleep on bare concrete, but they prefer a fresh, clean bed of hay. They fluff up the hay to keep it comfortable and soft, and they litter their pens as far as possible from their beds.

Pet Pointer

Garbage that is fed to a pig should be cooked first at 212 °F (100 °C). That will kill germs and parasites.

CIRCUS OF THE PIGS

Since they haven't any sweat glands,
pigs have to get wet to cool off when it's
hot outside. But they don't really need
mud baths. They enjoy a clean pond, a
river, or fine mists from a hose. So much
for calling that sloppy person a pig—
someone who lives like a pig is
pretty tidy!

Do you know anyone who eats like a
pig? If you do, you know a fairly
picky eater. Pigs do eat a lot, but
unlike cows, horses, and people, they
never overeat. In fact, if a pig is full,
you just can't make it eat another bite.

At first glance, it may not seem as if a pig is fussy about food. After all, it eats kitchen scraps, garden wastes, and even stray snakes down at the pond. If you watch a pig closely, however, you will see it poke through its food and search for its favorite tidbits.

Pigs like corn a lot. They also like freshly cut hay, potatoes, pumpkins, turnips, skim milk, buttermilk, and meal from cottonseed, flaxseed, and soybeans.

It's a Pet Fact

Pigs can eat most kinds of poisonous snakes without getting ill from the venom.

They'll eat garden scraps and kitchen scraps, too. They are also willing to eat commercially prepared pig feed, which provides all the nutrition they need, though it may not be their favorite snack. And they absolutely need fresh, clean water to drink.

How can you tell if a pig is doing well? Just look for a gleam in its eyes and a tight, springy curl in its tail.

Of course, any bright, healthy pig is bound to go looking for trouble. Even a common barnyard pig can teach itself to slide the bolt that locks its pen, so a pig's pen must be made well. It should be strong enough to withstand leaning, deep enough in the ground to withstand digging, and clean and cozy enough to make a pig want to stay.

To be comfortable, a pigpen should have a feed rack, a watering trough, and a rubbing post. It should also have a sheltered area where the pig can escape from the sun, wind, or rain. Shelters in cold climates should be insulated, and those in hot climates should have lots of ventilation.

To be a great home, a pigpen should have at least one human visitor who cares about the pig that lives there— someone as friendly, as smart, and as neat as a pig!

It's a Pet Fact

Pigs can be very helpful in gardens. If you scatter seeds, they can tread them in to just the right depth for planting. And even a medium-sized pig creates more than a ton of fertilizer each year.

Separating the Sheep from the Goats

Cory raced across the yard to the fenced-in pasture. It was her last day at the farm, and she wanted to say good-bye to her twin cousins, Andy and Alex. When she got to the gate, she stopped short. The two boys were dressed exactly alike. From a distance,

the sheep and goats all looked the same, too. Who was who? What was what?

Just then, both boys came running to greet her. Up close, she saw Andy's crooked grin and Alex's glasses.

"You two sure had me confused," she said. "And so did your animals."

A Pet Word to Know

A **ruminant** is a plant-eating animal that chews its food twice, such as a cow, sheep, or goat. It chews and swallows once. In its stomach, the chewed-up plants form a soft lump, or *cud.* Later, the animal brings the cud back up to chew again.

"Come on!" teased Andy. "Can't you tell a goat from a sheep?"

Cory blushed. "I can tell a sheep that needs shearing," she replied. "And when I see a goatee, I know I'm looking at a goat. But there must be more to it than that."

Andy relented. "Goats and sheep have a lot in common," he agreed. "They're both ruminants—they chew cud. And they need the same kinds of housing and fencing. That's why they can share the same pasture."

"They both give milk—though we use goat's milk more than sheep's milk," added Alex. "And both have coats we can wear. Did you know that mohair comes from goats?

"And then there's the matter of horns. Almost all goats have horns, but lots of sheep have them, too."

"Still, there are differences, too," said Andy. "For one, my goats are smarter than the sheep. They never get lost in their own pasture or get scared by the dogs."

"Maybe so," replied Alex. "But my sheep don't chew up shirts and sweaters or butt each other in the head just for fun!"

"True," laughed Andy. "Both animals get into trouble."

"Hey!" he yelled suddenly. "Get down, you two!" Alex and Cory turned just in time to see both a sheep and a goat—in the front seat of the family jeep.

178

Featured Creature

She wasn't good at spelling,
but she knew just what to say.
She didn't know geography
but traveled anyway.
Her knowledge of the rules
left much to be desired,
but when it came to following,
she never, ever tired.
She wasn't very bright,
but she was loyal, cute, and clean.
And still they turned her out of school:
Do "ewe" know who I mean?

ANSWER: Mary's little lamb

Pet Project

A Lamb You Can Take to School

Things You Need:

- worn sock
- two safety pins
- felt
- scissors
- glue
- yarn needle

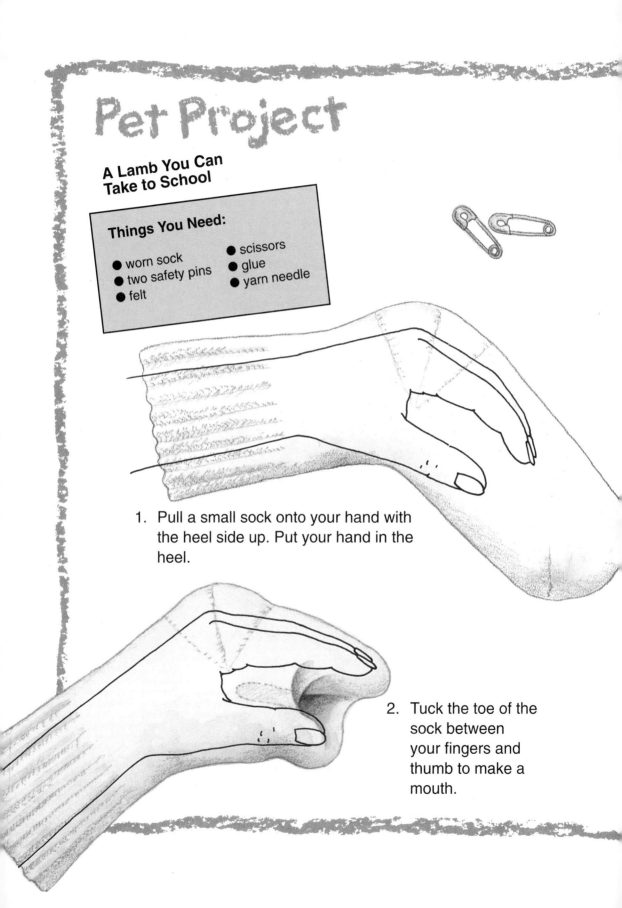

1. Pull a small sock onto your hand with the heel side up. Put your hand in the heel.

2. Tuck the toe of the sock between your fingers and thumb to make a mouth.

3. Turn the sock inside out. Pin the sides of the mouth together securely. Then turn the sock right side out and set it aside.

4. Cut out two ovals for eyes, a triangle for a nose, and two more triangles for ears. Glue them on.

5. Thread the needle with yarn and sew large loops on the top and sides of the head for wool. Ask for help with sewing if you need it.

6. Introduce your sock pet to the world!

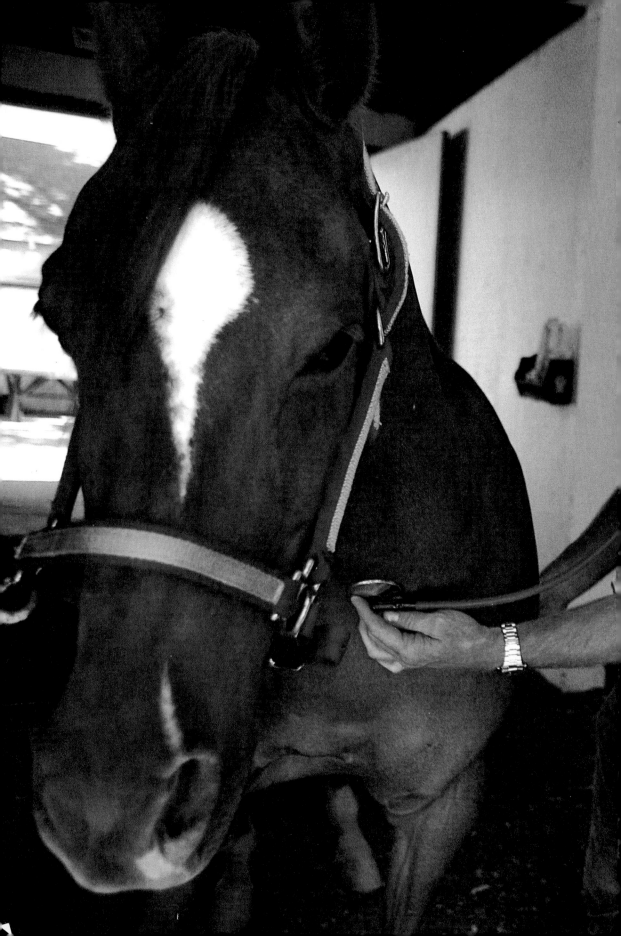

Penside Manner

What do you do when your pig catches cold?

No, it's not a riddle—it's a real live problem. And the answer is easy: You call a veterinarian! Animals, of course, don't like to be sick any more than we do. Veterinarians can help them get well and stay well.

The best way to keep an animal well is to protect it against disease. So veterinarians give farm animals yearly shots. They give horses deworming medicine, too, at least two times a year.

Many veterinarians also handle the simple tasks that keep animals healthy and clean. For example, veterinarians may *dock*, or trim, a lamb's tail to make it short and easy to keep clean. They also *float*, or file, horses' teeth. They give blood tests to cows and X rays to horses to make sure they are healthy and strong. They even give advice on nutrition and diet to help keep their patients in peak condition.

Still, even with lots of preventive action, animals sometimes become ill. A dairy cow, for example, can get very sick if its milking machine gets dirty. A veterinarian can prescribe antibiotics that kill the germs harming the cow.

Farm animals need vaccinations to protect them from diseases. Here an Australian veterinarian uses a special instrument to vaccinate a litter of piglets.

Veterinarians treat farm animals for many different illnesses. This veterinarian is putting powdered antibiotic into a cow's throat to cure an infection.

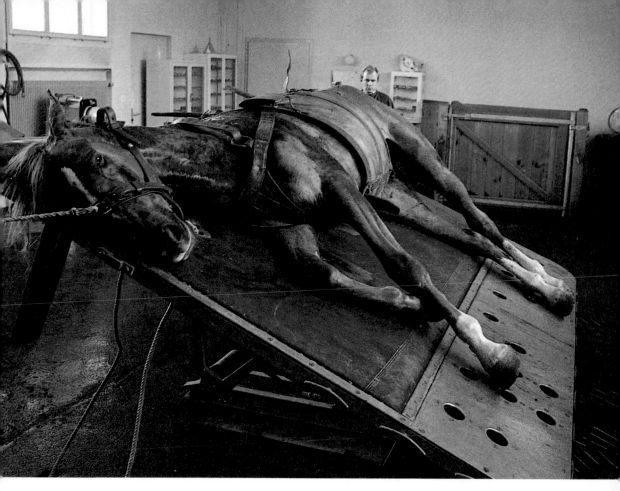

A special table like this one helps veterinarians treat lame horses. The veterinarian straps the standing horse to the table and then lowers it to a lying-down position.

Most horses become lame at some time in their lives. But if a veterinarian treats the lameness promptly, the horse can recover. To treat a lame horse, a veterinarian may strap it to a table that stands on its side. Once the horse is strapped on securely, the veterinarian turns a lever to tilt the tabletop right side up. That way, a lame horse can lie down on a table without being hoisted into the air.

If a horse is lame from an injured hoof, the veterinarian can clean and

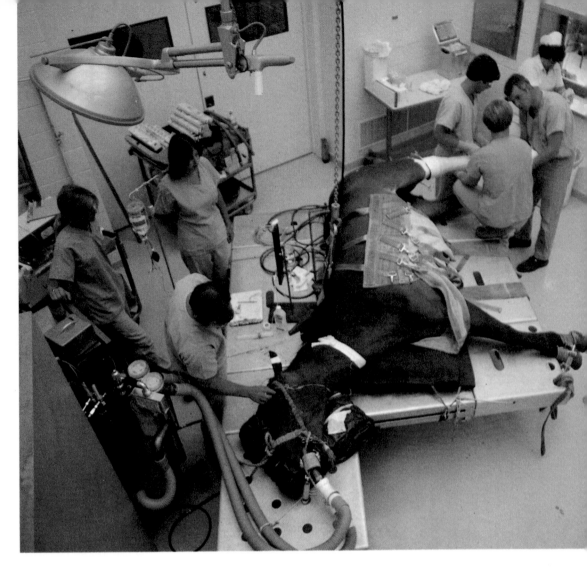

These veterinarians are performing surgery to repair a horse's broken leg. The anesthetic flows from a tank through a hose into the horse's mouth.

bandage the hoof, then give the animal medicine. If the lameness is due to a sprain or break, the veterinarian can wrap the hurt limb or put a cast on it.

When a farm animal needs surgery, a veterinarian can take care of that, too. The veterinarian gives the animal an anesthetic to make it sleep and then quickly operates to fix whatever is wrong. By the time the animal wakes up,

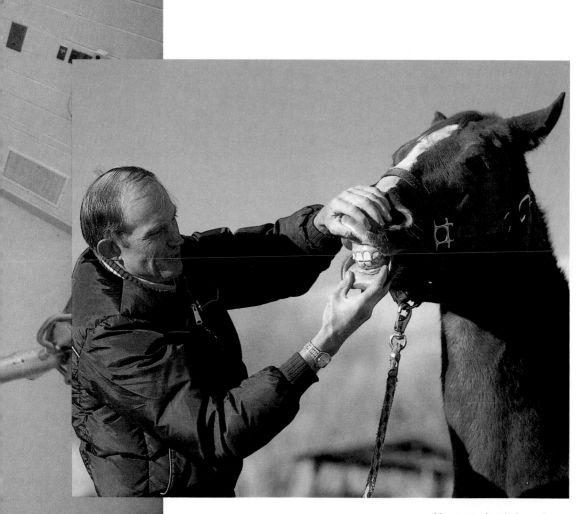

Horses don't brush their teeth every day like people do. But regular checkups keep their teeth and gums healthy.

the operation is over, and the animal is getting well.

Like many human doctors, farm veterinarians work day and night. They are on call for both emergencies and routine care. One way they are different from most other doctors is that they will make house calls! How does an animal doctor stay so dedicated? Now that is a real riddle!

Down at the Bison Corral

Mom says that many years ago, thousands of bison roamed all over North America. Now most of the great open spaces are big, settled ranches, like ours. But not all the ranchers raise cows and sheep. For example, our family keeps bison!

Once wild bison were hunted until they were almost gone. Ranchers saved some of them. Some of the bison that were saved were taken to national parks.

Now there are wild bison once again.

Bison also are raised on ranches for their meat, which is much leaner than beef. We graze them and feed them hay twice a day. And we give them treats of cracked corn.

Lots of ranchers today keep unusual stock. Our neighbors, the Garveys, raise llamas! Jeff Garvey says raising llamas is really carrying on an old tradition. Llamas were first tamed more than four thousand years ago. They provided meat, leather, wool, rope, fuel, candles, and tools made of bone. They also carried goods for trade.

A Pet Word to Know

Bison is the scientific name for the large, long-horned animals of North America that most people call buffalo.

The Garveys are raising most of their llamas to be pack animals and pets. That makes sense, because llamas are gentle and friendly.

Jeff says llamas can travel mountain paths no horse could ever handle. They can carry up to 130 pounds (59 kilograms) and travel from twelve to fifteen miles (19 to 24 kilometers) a day. They graze for their own food along the way. And they're so alert they spot wildlife that hikers would otherwise miss. They don't need much water, but the Garveys give them fresh water twice a day.

Jeff's mom is keeping some llamas to grow wool that she spins herself. Mrs. Garvey likes to handcraft rugs for the textile art gallery in Butte. She says that people all over the world borrow ideas for warmth and beauty from animals.

She says that ranchers in the Andes Mountains raise alpacas for their soft, strong wool. Alpacas are related to

llamas. Their wool is very fine, and now
people in the United States and Canada
are beginning to raise them. Mrs. Garvey
says ranchers in South Africa raise
ostriches for their feathers and hides.
Birds raised for their feathers aren't
killed—the feathers are plucked twice a
year.

By raising animals carefully, we can
help to protect them. I am proud that my
family raises and cares for animals that
have helped people in so many ways!

Pets Around the World

My Fishing
Feathered Friends

G reetings from Japan. My name is
Hiroshi. Beside me are my friends
the cormorants. I fish for a living, but I
use no hooks or nets. I have only the
flock. I have trained them to fish for me.

Cormorants are water birds that dive
beneath the water to catch fish to eat.
My cormorants were born on the sea
cliffs of Honshu, the largest island of

Japan. Bird catchers captured my birds and brought them to my village of Gifu.

After the birds came to live with me, I worked to earn their trust. I bathed and massaged them—even hand-fed them bits of carp, their favorite food. Now that my birds are tame, they repay me by doing what comes naturally—fishing.

As the sun sets, I take my boat down the Nagara River. The flock perches around me. At the front of the boat hangs a basket of burning sticks. The fish swim toward the light. Then my birds slip into the water.

The birds wear leather collars at the base of their necks. Attached to the collars are long leashes. I hold the ends of the leashes as the birds lower their heads into the water to look for fish.

When the birds spot a school of fish,
they dive. In the sea, with no leashes
around their necks, they easily could dive
more than one hundred feet (30 meters).
Soon, they splash back to the surface
with wriggling mouthfuls. Then they
swallow the fish whole. The birds dive
again and again until their long throats
are full. Finally, they return to the boat
and give the fish to me.

The fish stay in the birds' throats
because the snug collars keep them
there. I must adjust the collars carefully
every day. Sometimes, if the collars are
too loose, the birds pretend they can't
swallow. I'm fooled into thinking the

collars are tight enough. Then those rascals feast on the fish they catch instead of giving them to me! But most of the time, they are good birds and willing to share the fish they have caught.

When the cormorants have gathered enough fish, I draw them back into the boat. I loosen their collars and feed them carp. The birds eagerly gobble the food from my hand. It's a small reward for their tireless night of fishing.

I am honored to fish with my noble flock. They help me make my living as my parents and grandparents did. What more could I ask from friends?

A Kangaroo Survivor

Emma is a gray kangaroo that was born in the *outback,* or wilderness, of Australia. She began her life no bigger than your thumbprint. But nursing on rich milk in her mother's warm pouch, she grew quickly.

One morning, when Emma was about eight months old, her mother leaned over and loosened the muscles at the top of her pouch, and out flopped Emma. Emma let out a little frightened grunt and frantically tried to get back into the cozy pouch. But her mother stood upright and wouldn't let her in. She knew it was time for Emma to leave the pouch and join the other kangaroos in the mob.

Soon, Emma came to enjoy being outside her mother's pouch. There were all the other joeys to play with, and so many new things to explore. And besides, when Emma needed to rest or nurse, or when the wild dogs called *dingoes* were on the prowl, her mother would lean over and let her climb back in.

One day, the leader of their mob thumped a warning on the ground. Something even more dangerous than

Pet Words to Know

Mob is the name we use for a group of kangaroos.

A **joey** is a baby kangaroo.

dingoes was near—human hunters. The kangaroos scattered helter-skelter, and Emma's mother jumped in fright, leaping away at forty miles (65 kilometers) per hour. But the hunters chased her in a jeep. The mother wanted to lead them away from Emma, so she tipped Emma out of the pouch. Emma lay very still, and soon the hunters went away. But she never saw her mother again.

Luckily, some people who cared about kangaroos and wanted to protect them found Emma huddled in the brush along the road. The Australian government forbids keeping kangaroos as pets, but it permits people to raise an orphan like Emma until it can live on its own. So the people took Emma to a kangaroo orphanage. There, joeys that had lost their mothers were cared for until they were old enough to live on their own.

The people at the orphanage knew that cow's milk would make Emma sick. So they mixed a special formula and fed it to Emma in a baby bottle. As Emma grew, she also ate grass and low shrubs.

The people also knew that joeys that lived at the orphanage missed their mothers' pouches. So they hung a sack on

a clothesline for each of the joeys there.
Whenever Emma felt tired or frightened,
she crawled into her sack, just as she
used to crawl into her mother's pouch.
When the weather was cold, electric
heating pads kept the pouches warm.

After six months at the orphanage,
Emma was ready to leave. The people
released her in a wildlife preserve, where
hunters are not allowed. Now Emma
lives with a new mob and is raising a
joey of her own.

Fun and Games—
Dolphin Style

Imagine riding a wild dolphin. The dolphin's body is sleek and smooth. It feels kind of like a wet rubber raft. You hold onto the dolphin's fin, while the up-and-down strokes of its strong tail pull you through the shimmering waves. What an adventure!

Dolphins look and swim like fish. But they are mammals, just as human beings are. They have warm blood, breathe air, and give birth to live young. Some people today even believe that dolphins try to communicate with human beings.

Dolphins may sound like the magical animals in fairy tales, and riding a dolphin may seem like a crazy fantasy. But stories of children riding dolphins go back almost two thousand years. More recently, wild dolphins have been filmed playing with people. Some wild dolphins have become tourist attractions because they have stayed so long in one place.

One of these dolphins was called Opo. Opo spent a summer near a beach in New Zealand. Opo allowed swimmers to pet it and played with a beach ball they tossed to it. Opo formed a special bond with a thirteen-year-old girl named Jill Baker. Opo would recognize Jill even from behind, slip under her, and give her rides through the water.

Jill said that she thought Opo was especially friendly to her because she was always gentle with the dolphin. Also, she didn't rush to try to touch it, the way some swimmers did.

Perhaps one reason wild dolphins play
with people is that they are naturally
fun-loving. They often invent their own
games. Divers have seen wild dolphins
playing "keepaway" with bits of seaweed
and fish skin. Two dolphins in a marina
played for hours with a feather. They
placed it near a jet of water in the side of
the tank and then chased it as it shot
through the water. And wild dolphins are
often seen "surfing" on the waves created
by large ships.

The playful creativity of captive dolphins often surprises their trainers. Brenda was a dolphin at a New Zealand marina. A trainer arrived at her tank with a bat. Brenda had never before played baseball, but she immediately used her nose to toss a ball at the bat. The trainer was amazed because dolphins usually toss balls directly to people.

Later, the trainer expanded the game and added it to the dolphin show. Brenda pitched, and three other dolphins played in the outfield. Meanwhile, the trainer tried to reach home plate before the other dolphins got the ball back to Brenda. He didn't always make it, either.

It's a Pet Fact

Wild dolphins have been known to rescue swimmers in trouble. One such dolphin, a friendly female, appeared regularly off the coast of a small seaport in Spain. One onlooker could not resist getting into the water with her, even though he was not a strong swimmer. Soon his legs cramped and he shouted for help. The dolphin swam up to him and kept his head above the water until help arrived.

Somalo, an Indian Mongoose

Meet my pet mongoose, Somalo. Mongooses are known for their fierceness with snakes. Somalo is no different. He is a brave and clever mongoose, but I still worry when I see him rush to fight a snake.

I suppose I need not be concerned. My father tells me that the snake's venom cannot hurt a mongoose very much. Anyway, Somalo leaps and dodges so quickly that snakes don't have a chance to bite him.

My pet seems fearless when he faces a snake in the garden outside. Like a bolt of lightning, he darts at the snake's neck and bites. Again and again he bites, until the snake dies. Then Somalo eats it.

Somalo is fierce with snakes but like a kitten with me. Inside the house, he naps peacefully on my shoulder. Sometimes he passes his tail under my chin and tickles me. Then I laugh until the tears come.

I give Somalo bits of meat when the hunting is poor, but he enjoys eggs more. When I give him an egg, he throws it under his body and between his hind legs and cracks it against the wall. Then he dips his front paw in the yolk and laps it up as if it were honey. My mother doesn't like it when I feed raw eggs to Somalo because he makes such a mess.

The best trained mongoose I have seen belongs to the snake charmer in my village. People gather as the man waves his flute to lure the cobra from its basket. They gasp when the mongoose and the cobra do their dance of death. The snake sways and hisses, and the mongoose makes wicked clicking noises.

But the snake charmer's mongoose has been trained never to attack the cobra. Still, the people stare breathlessly, waiting to see which will win—the master's training or the mongoose's nature. After all, the mongoose may be friendly with people, but it remains a wild creature.

Featured Creature

He sees a scaly creature in the grass,
With a flickering tongue and eyes like
    polished glass.
It's tricky, strong, and quick,
But *ricky-ticky-tick*—
He will never, never, ever let it pass!

Just wait until it tries to slither by!
Ricky-ticky-tick will be his cry,
And if it should try to bite,
It's in for quite a fight—
He'll bounce and pounce and
    make that snakeskin fly!

Who is he?

ANSWER: Rikki-Tikki-Tavi!

The Camel: A Desert Pet

I met Raishu on her birthday. Or I should say, "birthnight." She was born just after midnight. The bright silver moon shone in a perfect black desert sky, and its light twinkled on the sand. My people are Tuareg, and we are *nomads* in the Sahara. This means that we move about constantly, seeking pasture for our herds of livestock.

Raishu was a newborn *dromedary*, or one-humped camel, and she had legs

almost as long as her mother's. She stood
up before she was three hours old.

Raishu and her mother could not rest
long after her birth. My family and their
camels were in the middle of a journey,
and we had to continue. Raishu could
stand, but she was still shaky. So my
father wrapped her in a net and placed
her on the back of another camel to carry.

A mother camel fusses and wanders
away if she cannot see her calf. So

Raishu's mother followed behind the other camel. I walked beside the mother. Watching Raishu made my morning-long walk seem short.

Raishu and I became special friends. By the time she was a week old, she was galloping about our camp. When she got tired, she knelt beside me and rested her head in my lap. She enjoyed being scratched. Sometimes she would nibble my face the way her mother nibbled hers.

For two weeks, Raishu's only food was her mother's milk. Then I began to feed her dates and grain. Now Raishu finds her own food in the desert—seeds, pods, and even the thorns that tear our clothes if we pass near them.

Raishu can eat such foods because her mouth and tongue are tough. But these are not the only things that help Raishu survive so well. Even her feet were made for desert life. A wide pad covers the bottom of each foot. The pads keep Raishu's feet from sinking in the sand.

Sand in the wind can be a bigger nuisance than sand on the ground. Again, Raishu comes prepared. During a sandstorm, she can shut her nostrils so no sand blows in her nose. Her long

lashes keep sand out of her eyes. And Raishu's tiny ears are filled with hair, so no sand can get into them, either.

Like other camels, Raishu can go for months without a drink in the cooler part of the year. She gets water from the plants she eats. Also, she hardly sweats and passes little water in her wastes.

But when a well is nearby, a thirsty camel smells the water and races to it. A grown camel can drink thirty-five gallons (135 liters) in a few minutes. Raishu can't drink that fast, but she's working on it.

Pet Project

Spin Around the World Game

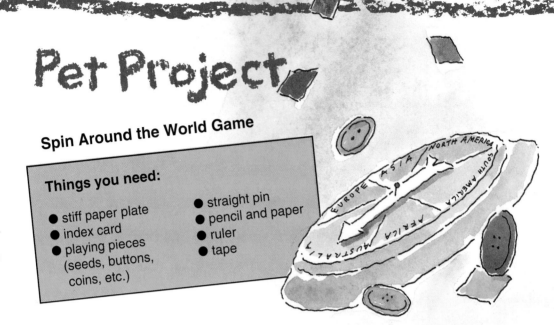

Things you need:

- stiff paper plate
- index card
- playing pieces (seeds, buttons, coins, etc.)
- straight pin
- pencil and paper
- ruler
- tape

Take a spin around the world of animals!

1. First, make a spinner. Turn the paper plate bottom-side-up. Draw lines to divide it into six sections, like a pie. Label the sections *Africa, Asia, Australia, Europe, North America,* and *South America.*

2. Cut an arrow from the index card. Push the pin through the arrow and into the center of the paper plate. Ask a grown-up to bend the pin and tape the point so it does not stick anyone.

3. Give each player a pile of playing pieces.

4. Have each player make a game card like the one shown on the next page.

5. Spend a few minutes looking over the map and at the pictures of animals on pages 216 and 217. Try to recall as many animals as you can.

Now you are ready to play. Here are the rules:

1. One player is the first map-keeper. He or she turns to the map on pages 216 and 217.

2. The player to the right of the map-keeper spins first. When the arrow stops on the name of a continent, the player names an animal that lives there. The map-keeper tells whether the spinning player is correct.

3. If the answer is correct, the player places a playing piece on the game card in a square under that continent.

4. The spinning player passes the spinner to the player on his or her right and becomes the map-keeper for the next player's turn. Repeat step number two. Note: a player may not name an animal named on the previous turn.

5. On the game card, players try to fill a row across by naming one animal from each continent, or fill a row down by naming six animals from one continent. The first player to fill a row wins.

6. More advanced players may name animals not pictured on the map if they can prove that their answer is correct with a book or dictionary.

AFRICA   ASIA   AUSTRALIA   EUROPE   NORTH AMERICA   SOUTH AMERICA

1
2
3
4
5

NORTH AMERICA

Sea Otter

Gray Wolf

Canada Goose

Raccoon

King Snake

Desert Tortoise

White-tailed Deer

Wild Turkey

Canary

SOUTH AMERICA

Woolly Monkey

Piranha

Galapagos Tortoise

Llama

Toucan

Green Iguana

Macaw

SPIN AROUND THE WORLD

Cavy

Pets Outside the Door

Butch Speaks Out!

They scamper along leafy branches. They peep out from holes in front lawns. They flit on the wing from tree to tree. Who are they? They're the animals that share our neighborhoods. And often, they are unnoticed and unappreciated. But if Butch D'Squirrel, president of Wild Pals Action League (WiPAL), has his way, things will change.

"There is more than one way to have a pet," says D'Squirrel. "Pups and kitties are meant to be owned and cuddled. But there are other animals that we call 'wild pets.' People do not own these animals. They appreciate them by observing them in their natural surroundings."

D'Squirrel's office is tucked in the trunk of a hollow tree in City Park. He

Wild
Pets
Leave us
and
Love us!

"We wild animals may not like being caged or cuddled. But we *deserve* to be seen and appreciated. We can teach people a lot."

Butch D'Squirrel

works day in and day out to spread the WiPAL word, sitting among the stacks of letters and leaflets that clutter his desk. He has some pointers for those who want to learn to enjoy wild pets. "To start with, you can observe us," D'Squirrel says. "Certain kinds of animals seem to look and act in much the same ways. But they actually may have different habits.

Pet Pointer

Never chase, corner, tease, or strike wild animals. That's no way to be a friend. Besides, with claws, quills, a stinger, or teeth, an animal may strike back to defend itself.

"For example, many people think all birds are alike. Take sparrows and swallows. Almost anytime, anywhere, you can go outside and see sparrows pecking away on the ground. But have you ever seen a swallow on the ground? No way. Their feet don't work well on the ground. They spend almost all their time on the wing, catching insects to eat."

Photography is another way to get acquainted with your wild neighbors, according to D'Squirrel. "Go ahead, snap away. We love that kind of attention." He also suggests sketching neighborhood animals. "It's an even more personal way to preserve your experience of wild pets."

Mount your sketches and photos in a scrapbook and jot down notes along with them. "Or describe what you see us doing in a wildlife journal," D'Squirrel says.

You can feed animal neighbors, too. D'Squirrel cautions, however, to make sure that you put out only the right kinds of foods. "Veterinarians, zoo officials, or books can give you pointers," he advises.

It doesn't matter how you choose to get to know your animal neighbors better. "Any way is okay," says Butch D'Squirrel. "Just do it today!"

Wildlife Hospital

What happens when a wild animal gets sick? Unfortunately, no doctors are on call in the wild, and many sick wild animals never get well. But once in a while, a kindhearted human finds a sick or injured mammal, bird, or reptile or an orphaned baby animal and takes it to a wildlife hospital.

It could be an owl, fawn, badger, otter, chipmunk, groundhog, or even a skunk. Let's go inside the hospital to see what happens next.

First, the animal is taken to the examining table. If it is injured, the veterinarian treats it. The veterinarian hurries, for it is probably cold and scared. If the animal is a baby, the doctor cradles it under his or her arm or close to the neck for warmth. The doctor may place a grown animal near a heat lamp or in a box with a heating pad under it, making sure that the animal doesn't get too warm.

Next, the doctor makes certain the animal is not *dehydrated*. An animal is dehydrated when it does not have enough water in the tissues of its body. A dehydrated animal is in great danger of dying. So the veterinarian gives the animal a shot or fluids through a tube in its mouth.

When the animal is warm, calm, and no longer dehydrated, feeding begins. Veterinarians feed baby animals nutritious formulas made especially for each type of animal. Depending on the baby's size and strength, the doctor feeds it with a syringe, medicine dropper, or baby bottle. Older animals are able to feed themselves. Mammals eat such

Pet Pointer

Before you take a baby animal to the wildlife hospital, make sure it is really an orphan. Many animal mothers leave their babies alone while they search for food. If the baby seems comfortable, do not disturb it. Its mother probably will be back soon. If you are concerned about the baby, you can check on it the next day to make sure it is all right.

225

foods as meat, insects, nuts, acorns, berries, vegetables, wheat, oats, and wild grasses.

Veterinarians say that animals raised in captivity must learn to recognize their own kind if they are to survive in the wild. So the animal spends several weeks recovering with others like it in a small box or cage lined with soft, warm cloth. And, to give the animals a feel for the outdoors, the doctor takes their cages outside often.

Wildlife veterinarians know that homes and hospitals do not make the best homes for wild animals. So when the

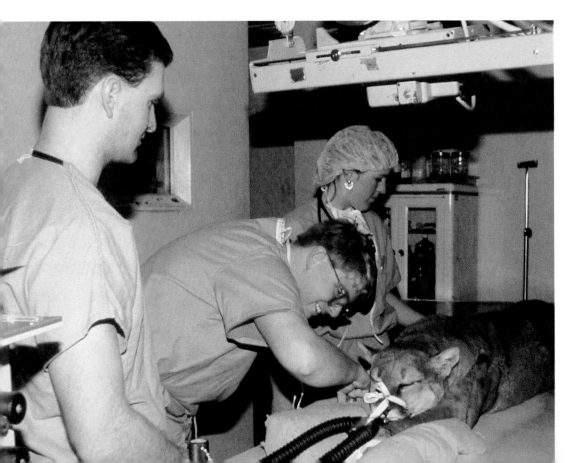

animal is finally strong and healthy, the veterinarian scouts out the perfect spot to set it free. The area should have the right kinds of food and shelter for the animal.

At the perfect place at the perfect time, the veterinarian opens the cage and the animal is free. What a feeling—to care for ailing animals until they are well enough to scurry, fly, or crawl away on their own!

I'm Glad You're My Neighbor

No matter where in the world you call home, chances are you share your backyard with a variety of outdoor "pets." Let's travel throughout North America and meet some boys and girls and their animal neighbors.

Deciduous forests—those with trees that lose their leaves in the fall—cover most of New Hampshire. Just beyond Ben and Gary's backyard is a forestful of wonderful creatures. Their woodland pals include squirrels, chipmunks, mice, skunks, deer, frogs, foxes, hawks, garter snakes, weasels, rabbits, salamanders, and all kinds of birds and insects.

One of the brothers' favorite things to do in summer is to collect insects and watch their behavior. Their prize pet was a fat, green caterpillar that turned into a beautiful, soft, reddish-brown Cecropia (*suh KRO pee uh*) moth with wings six inches (15 centimeters) across. They set the moth free on Gary's birthday.

A Pet Word to Know

A **habitat** is a community of wild creatures. Each habitat has a particular climate and type of land. Different habitats are home to different types of animals and plants.

Beau and his family live in Louisiana in a lush, warm wetland called a *bayou* (*BY oo*). When Beau is not in school, he takes his dog, Tinou, and they explore the bayou in his family's boat. Sunlight slices through the trees in golden streaks as Beau glides quietly along. Sleek minks swim through the water, hunting frogs, crayfish, and fish. Shimmery water birds called purple gallinules step daintily on floating plants, while alligators and snapping turtles prowl under the water.

Imagine a backyard habitat with almost no trees, where swaying grasses go on for miles. This land is called a *prairie*. Angie rides with her father to check the fences on their ranch in South Dakota. Pronghorn bound out of their way, and turkey vultures perch on the power lines. Angie laughs to see the prairie dogs play, kissing and nuzzling one another in their prairie dog towns. Burrowing owls bob their heads and duck into abandoned prairie dog holes when Angie and her father get too close.

Susannah and her brother Jesse love
to discover the many creatures that
share their desert backyard in Arizona.
Once in a while, a spiked, chubby horned
lizard or a big, hairy tarantula creeps
into the backyard. Speedy brown birds
called roadrunners dash by on their
strong legs, and purple-headed Costa's
hummingbirds visit their father's
flowers. At night, Susannah and Jesse
fall asleep to the sound of coyotes calling
in the hills.

Michele lives with her parents in a cozy home in Echo Bay on the tundra of Canada's Northwest Territories. It stays cool there the year around. Patches of grass and trees only about one foot (30 centimeters) tall tremble in the wind.

In the short summer, insects flourish, and all kinds of birds arrive to raise their young. Water birds, including Arctic loons, mergansers (*muhr GAN suhrz*), teals, and horned grebes gather by the thousands on Great Bear Lake. Michele throws grain near the house to attract Canada geese. A special treat is a glimpse of a majestic gyrfalcon (*JUHR FAWL kuhn*) circling on a cloudless day. Sturdy musk oxen and caribou, as well as Arctic hares and lemmings, also share Michele's tundra home.

Near their home on the California coast, Randy and Melissa have fun exploring the tide pools, with their sea anemones (*uh NEHM uh neez*), starfish, crabs, and little fish. Offshore, sea otters play in the kelp, and blubbery elephant seals sprawl on the rocks. Flocks of gulls make a racket when Randy and Melissa throw them scraps of bread.

Where do you live? North or south, east or west, hot or cold, wet or dry, fascinating creatures are everywhere. Think about the animals that visit your own backyard, and maybe you'll find friends you didn't know you had!

Guardians at the Gate

Beth and Brian dreamed of being explorers. All they needed was a real expedition.

"I have a lot of helpers in the garden," Mrs. Chumleigh, their neighbor, said. "They're insect predators that control garden pests. Walk with me and we'll watch them in action."

The backyard seemed very still and quiet. "Where do we begin?" asked Brian.

"We can start right here at my lovely hydrangea," said Mrs. Chumleigh. She parted the leaves to reveal a strange-looking mass on the branch. "Look at this. What do you see?"

"A light brown blob stuck to a stick," Brian answered.

"That's what it appears to be, Brian. But it's more than that. It's a sac of about three hundred eggs. That praying mantis laid it," Mrs. Chumleigh said.

Beth and Brian jumped in fright when they laid eyes on the long, green insect with folded front legs peering at them from the top of a hydrangea blossom. "Nothing to fear," Mrs. Chumleigh said.

"She won't hurt you. She eats all kinds of harmful insects. And when her young hatch in the spring, they'll help her."

"Boy, with all those praying mantises around, you won't have any insect pests," observed Beth.

"One would think so," Mrs. Chumleigh sighed. "Unfortunately, mantises often get carried away and eat one another. So the young run away in search of their own gardens to protect."

"Yuck," said Brian. "Insect predators aren't very nice."

"They just do what is natural, Brian. And some are quite charming. Why don't we go over to my roses and meet the ladybugs?" suggested Mrs. Chumleigh.

"Ladybugs are so cute. Are they really fierce predators?" asked Beth as they watched a crowd of round, red bugs with black dots scurrying along the stems.

"Oh yes," replied Mrs. Chumleigh. "They tirelessly gobble up aphids so the aphids don't gobble up my roses. By the way, do you like my roses? I'm so proud of my red pinocchios. My husband, Melvin, planted them when. . . ."

Just then a loud buzzing startled them. A gleaming green dragonfly, shaped like a helicopter, zoomed into

view. "Oh, an unexpected visit from Mr. Darningneedle," said Mrs. Chumleigh. "See how he carries his legs like a basket? He collects lots and lots of mosquitoes that way—mosquitoes that would otherwise dine on your blood."

"Thank you, Mr. Darningneedle!" Beth called.

"Shhh!" Mrs. Chumleigh said. "Now is your chance to learn about the royal family of garden predators. Beth and Brian, meet Queen Garden Spider."

A fat, yellow-and-black spider rested elegantly in a web that hung between two sunflowers. Her body was nearly the size of a half dollar.

"She traps countless insect pests in her web," said Mrs. Chumleigh. "And her relatives help, too—jumping spiders, lynx spiders, and wolf spiders, to name a few. If it weren't for the spiders, who knows what my garden would be? In fact, have I told you about the time thrips attacked Mr. Chumleigh's mums? He tried—"

Just then, the clanging of a bell interrupted Mrs. Chumleigh's story.

"Must be dinnertime," Brian said. "We'd really like to stay and hear about the mums, Mrs. C."

"Sure would, Mrs. C.," Beth added with a frown. "But we have to get going."

"We're having liver and creamed peas!" said Brian.

"Why, that's Mr. Chumleigh's favorite dish!" cried Mrs. Chumleigh. But Beth and Brian didn't hear. They had already disappeared like two darting dragonflies through the garden gate.

Featured Creature

She wove a round web
of strong silken thread.
To save her friend's skin
she put some words in
that said just what had to be said.

It hung in the barn
on Zuckerman's farm.
Though the web wasn't big,
and said simply, "Some pig,"
it kept humble Wilbur from harm.

Who is the weaver?

Answer: Charlotte

Pet Puzzler

Panorama of Backyard Pets

Can you find the following animal neighbors in the illustration below?

praying mantis	garter snake	butterfly	spider
purple martin	chipmunk	raccoon	rabbit
hummingbird	dragonfly	ladybug	frog
		squirrel	bee

Books to Read

There are many fine books on pets and pet care and on the lives of wild animals. This list is just a sample. You may find these books and others like them at your school or public library.

Ages 5-8

Cats Know Best by Colin Eisler (Dial, 1988)

Cats are curious creatures! Read this book to find out about what cats do and why they do it.

Frogs and Toads by Kate Petty (Franklin Watts, 1985)

Enjoy the pretty artwork in this book and get answers to many of your questions about frogs and toads. You might also want to read a book called *Spiders* by the same author.

Gerbil Pets and Other Small Rodents by Ray Broekel (Childrens Press, 1983)

Learn how to care for your gerbil, hamster, guinea pig, or mouse. And for advice on caring for your underwater friends, read *Tropical Fish* by the same author.

A Horse Named Paris by Lynn Sonberg (Bradbury, 1986)

Meet Amanda as she cares for her horse, Paris, and learn about all the special things a girl and her horse do together.

How Dog Began by Pauline Baynes (Holt, 1986)

This is the story of Curr, a wolf cub adopted by a group of people in ancient times. Curr helps the people in many ways and becomes the first tame dog.

My First Kitten by Rosmarie Hausherr (Four Winds, 1985)

Seven-year-old Adam adopts a kitten and gets a new friend to care for and love.

To Love a Dog by Colleen Stanley Bare (Dodd, Mead, 1987)

Color photographs show what the many different breeds of dogs look like. Simple facts about caring for dogs also are included.

Ages 9-12

101 Questions and Answers About Pets and People by Ann Squire (Macmillan, 1988)

Here are some answers to questions young people have about their pet birds, cats, dogs, fish, hamsters, horses, and many others.

All Wild Creatures Welcome: The Story of a Wildlife Rehabilitation Center by Patricia Curtis (Lodestar, 1985)

Caring for orphaned, sick, or injured animals is challenging, but important. Learn about the people who do this interesting job and what you should do if you ever find a wild animal in trouble.

Choosing Your Pet by Mark McPherson (Troll, 1985)

What kind of pet is right for you—a cat, dog, turtle, mouse, parrot, fish, or something else? This book describes the special needs of a wide variety of pets and the pleasures they bring. Other books by the same author include *Caring for Your Cat, Caring for Your Dog,* and *Caring for Your Fish.*

Close Encounters with Insects and Spiders by James B. Nardi (Iowa State University Press, 1988)

Discover the crawly critters that share your world! This book classifies familiar insects and spiders according to where they live. It's a valuable companion on a bug safari through your own backyard!

The Complete Frog: A Guide for the Very Young Naturalist by Elizabeth Lacey (Lothrop, Lee, & Shepard, 1989)

You'll find a wealth of useful and interesting information on frogs—including useful advice on caring for your pet frogs and tadpoles—in this book.

Dogs: All About Them by Alvin and Virginia Silverstein (Lothrop, Lee, & Shepard, 1986)

This book has everything you need to know about dog breeds, dog history, dog care, dogs that work for people, and wild dog relatives.

Dogs on Duty by Catherine O'Neill (National Geographic Society, 1988)

Dogs help people in many ways, doing real jobs—from herding sheep to helping police officers. Read all about working dogs in this photo-packed book.

Dolphins and Porpoises by Dorothy Hinshaw Patent (Holiday House, 1987)

These graceful, intelligent animals are forever fascinating. This book discusses both wild dolphins and dolphins and their relationships with people.

Horsemanship: Basics for Beginners by Evelyn Pervier (Messner, 1984)

Here's an introduction to horse ownership, including

information on types of horses, choosing a horse that's right for you, and caring for a horse. Also try two other books in this series by the same author: *Basics for Intermediate Riders* and *Basics for More Advanced Riders.*

How to Raise Butterflies by E. Jaediker Norsgaard (Dodd, Mead, 1988)

All you need to know to be an honest-to-goodness "butterfly farmer" is covered in this book.

Life in a Tidal Pool by Alvin and Virginia Silverstein (Little, Brown, 1990)

A tidal pool is like a lovely ocean in miniature. Take a walk along the seashore and study the various creatures that live in this unique habitat.

The Llama by Gail LaBonte (Dillon Press, 1989)

Llamas are intelligent and gentle creatures that are easy to train. Their soft wool also can be used to make many useful items. Read about these and other reasons why llamas are becoming popular pets in North America today.

Rabbits by Ann and Michael Sproule (Bookwright, 1988)

Written especially for kids who want to own a bunny or two, this book has all you need to know about the joys—and the many responsibilities—of rabbit care.

Sea Otters by Ruth Ashby (Aladdin, 1990)

Frisky and frolicking, the sea otter is many people's favorite floating friend. You'll be swept away by the color photos as you read about the life and habits of these special animals.

New Words

Here are some words you have read in this book. Some of them may be new to you. Next to each word you'll see how to say the word: **dromedary** (DRAHM uh DEHR ee). The part in large capital letters is said the loudest. The part in small capitals is said a little bit loud. The part in small letters is said the least loud. One or two sentences tell the word's meaning as it is used in this book.

algae (AL jee) Simple living things that live in oceans, rivers, lakes, ponds, and moist soil. Some algae have only a single cell. Seaweeds are large, many-celled algae that live in the ocean.

amphibian (am FIHB ee uhn) A kind of cold-blooded animal that has moist skin without scales and lays its eggs in water. Young amphibians live in the water, but as they grow they change form and later live on land. Frogs, toads, newts, and salamanders are amphibians.

aquarium (uh KWAIR ee uhm) 1. A pond, tank, or glass bowl that holds living water plants and animals, especially fish. 2. A building used for showing collections of living water animals and plants.

booster shot (BOOS tuhr shaht) A vaccination that doctors give to make the benefit of an earlier vaccination last longer.

brine shrimp (bryn shrihmp) A tiny, shelled animal found in salt water. Brine shrimp are used as fish food.

calcium (KAL see uhm) A chemical element that is a soft, silvery-white material. It is a part of limestone, chalk, milk, bones, shells, and teeth. It is an important mineral in the diets of people and animals.

cavy (KAY vee) A South American rodent that is short-tailed or tailless and burrows in the ground. The guinea pig is the best-known type of cavy.

chlorine (KLAWR een) A greenish-yellow, bad-smelling gas that is very irritating to the nose, throat, and lungs. Small amounts of chlorine are used to kill germs in tap water. Chlorine is poisonous to some water animals and must be removed from tap water before it can be used in an aquarium.

cud (kuhd) A lump of partly digested food brought back from the first stomach of a cow, camel, sheep, or goat. Cud comes up so that the animal can chew it a second time more slowly.

cuttlebone (KUHT uhl BOHN) The hard shell found inside a squidlike animal called a *cuttlefish*. It is used as food for cage birds.

domesticated (duh MEHS tuh kayt uhd) Tamed, no longer wild. Dogs, cows, horses, and camels are domesticated animals.

dromedary (DRAHM uh DEHR ee) A swift camel with one hump and short hair, found in parts of India, Arabia, and northern Africa. Dromedaries are used for riding and carrying goods.

environment (ehn VY ruhn muhnt) The conditions of things, such as air, water, soil, plants, and animals, that affect the way living things grow and develop.

fluorescent lamp (FLOO uh REHS uhnt lamp) An electric lamp made up of a glass tube coated inside with a special material and filled with gas. It gives off light without much heat and is therefore good for use in aquariums and terrariums.

game (gaym) Wild animals, birds, or fish that people hunt or catch for food or sport.

gills (gihlz) The red, feathery organs near the head that a fish, tadpole, or other water animal uses to breathe. Oxygen passes into the animal's blood through the thin walls of the gills, and carbon dioxide passes out.

groom (groom) To rub down, brush, and generally take care of a horse, cat, or dog.

housetrain (HOWS trayn) To train a dog, cat, or other pet not to relieve itself in the house; to housebreak.

ich (ihk) A disease of aquarium fish in which small white specks appear on the fins and body. Ich is caused by a tiny, one-celled swimming creature that burrows under the fish's skin.

kelp (kehlp) A kind of large, brown, tough seaweed. A kind of giant kelp found in the Pacific Ocean has stems that can grow more than 150 feet (46 meters) long.

larva (LAHR vuh) An early form of some kinds of animals that is different from the adult form. A larva must go through a change to become like the parent.

migrate (MY grayt) To go from one place to another when the seasons change. Most birds migrate to warmer climates to spend the winter.

mohair (MOH hair) Cloth made from the long, silky hair of the Angora goat.

newt (noot *or* nyoot) A small salamander with a flattened tail that lives in water for part of its life.

parasite (PAR uh syt) An animal or plant that lives and feeds on another living thing, called a *host*. Some parasites are very harmful to their host plant or animal.

reptile (REHP tuhl *or* REHP tyl) A kind of cold-blooded animal that has a backbone and breathes with lungs, and usually has skin covered with scales or plates. Snakes, turtles, and alligators are reptiles.

rodent (ROH duhnt) A kind of animal that has front teeth that continue to grow and that are used for gnawing wood or other tough material. Guinea pigs, hamsters, mice, and squirrels are rodents.

salamander (SAL uh MAN duhr) A cold-blooded animal shaped like a lizard but related to frogs and toads. It has moist, smooth skin, four short legs, and usually a long tail. It lives in water and damp places.

saliva (suh LY vuh) A clear liquid made by glands in the mouth and cheeks. It keeps the mouth moist, helps in chewing and swallowing, and starts the digestion of food.

stethoscope (STEHTH uh skohp) An instrument used by doctors to listen to sounds in the heart, lungs, or other parts of the body.

suet (SOO iht) Hard fat found around the kidneys and loins of certain animals, especially cattle and sheep. It is used as food for wild birds.

tadpole (TAD pohl) A very young frog or toad at the stage when it has gills and a long tail and lives in water; a polliwog.

territorial (TEHR uh TAWR ee uhl) A word used to describe an animal that claims an area, or *territory*, where it lives and raises its young, and that defends the area from other animals.

tubifex worm (TOO buh fehks wurm) A small, red worm that is used as food for tropical fish and other water pets. Tubifex worms make tubes to live in and are often found in muddy water.

vaccination (VAK suh NAY shuhn) A special medicine given to protect people and animals from getting certain diseases.

venom (VEHN uhm) The poison of some snakes, spiders, scorpions, lizards, and insects.

Illustration Acknowledgments

The publishers of *Childcraft* gratefully acknowledge the courtesy of the following photographers, agencies, and organizations for illustrations in the volume. When all the illustrations for a sequence of pages are from a single source, the inclusive page numbers are given. Credits should be read from left to right, top to bottom, on their respective pages. All illustrations are the exclusive property of the publishers of *Childcraft* unless names are marked with an asterisk (*). Special pet symbols by Steven D. Mach.

Cover:	Aristocrat and Standard Bindings - Ed Simpson, TSW/Chicago Ltd.* Discovery Binding - Lydia Halverson Heritage Binding - © Reynolds Photography*; Yoshi Miyake; Pat & Robin DeWitt; Jean Cassels; Lydia Halverson; Pat & Robin DeWitt; Lydia Halverson; Pat & Robin DeWitt; Dennis Hockerman
1:	Dennis Hockerman
2-3:	Lydia Halverson
4-5:	Joan Holub; Jared D. Lee
6-7:	Jared D. Lee; Yoshi Miyake; Paul Meisel
8-9:	Lydia Halverson
10-11:	© Norvia Behling*
12-13:	Joan Holub
14-15:	Joan Holub; Reynolds Photography*
16-17:	Joan Holub; © Norvia Behling*; © Norvia Behling*
18-19:	Lydia Halverson
20-21:	Steven D. Mach; © Tom Tracy, Third Coast Stock*; © Norvia Behling*
22-23:	© Margot Conte, Animals Animals*; © Norvia Behling*
24-27:	Jean Cassels
28-31:	Joan Holub
32-33:	Steven D. Mach, © Gary Cameron, *Sports Illustrated**
34-35:	Jared D. Lee; Prehistoric painting located at Sefar on the Tassili N'ajjer Plateau, Algeria (Douglas Mazonowicz Gallery of Prehistoric Paintings, New York City)*; Yukon Tourist Bureau*
36-37:	© Reynolds Photography*; Jared D. Lee; © Penny G. Sullivan, American Rescue Dog Association*
38-39:	© Prescott-Allen, Animals Animals*; Canine Companions for Independence*; Jared D. Lee
40-41:	© Norvia Behling*
42-43:	© Norvia Behling*; Jean Cassels; Jean Cassels; World Book photo
44-45:	Jean Cassels; World Book photos
46-47:	Jean Cassels; © Norvia Behling*; Jean Cassels; © Mike and Moppet Reed, Animals Animals*
48-49:	Lydia Halverson; © Norvia Behling*
50-51:	Lydia Halverson; © Norvia Behling*
52-53:	Lydia Halverson; © Norvia Behling*
54-55:	Steven D. Mach; Field Museum of Natural History*
56-57:	Steven D. Mach
58-59:	Steven D. Mach; Detail of illustration by S. John Tenniel from the first edition, 1865, of *Alice's Adventures in Wonderland* by Lewis Carroll (Granger Collection)*
60-61:	Gwen Connelly; © Norvia Behling*
62-63:	© Norvia Behling*; Gwen Connelly
64-69:	Joan Holub
70-71:	TSW/Chicago Ltd.*
72-73:	Eldon Doty
74-75:	Robert Maier, Animals Animals*; Eldon Doty; Norvia Behling*; Eldon Doty
76-77:	Robert Maier, Animals Animals*; Eldon Doty
78-81:	Hal Just
82-85:	Paul Meisel
86-87:	Lydia Halverson; Isabelle Francais
88-91:	Lydia Halverson
92-93:	Lydia Halverson; Illustration from *The Tale of Peter Rabbit* by Beatrix Potter. © Frederick Warne and Co., 1902, 1987. By permission of Frederick Warne.*
94-95:	© Blair Seitz, Photo Researchers*
96-97:	Yoshi Miyake
98-99:	Tony Bucci*
100-101:	Lydia Halverson
102-103:	Lydia Halverson; Payne/Anderson, Third Coast Stock*
104-109:	Jared D. Lee

110-111:	Pat & Robin DeWitt
112-113:	Peabody Hotel*
114-119:	Yoshi Miyake
120-125:	Pat & Robin DeWitt
126-127:	Peter Brandt
128-133:	Dennis Hockerman
134-135:	Hal Just
136-137:	Jared D. Lee
138-139:	© Alvin E. Staffan, Photo Researchers*; Jared D. Lee
140-141:	William J. Jahoda, Photo Researchers*; © Alvin E. Staffan, Photo Researchers*
142-143:	Yoshi Miyake
144-145:	© Jim Morrill, Third Coast Stock*
146-147:	John F. Eggert; Donald Moss and Colin Newman, Bernard Thornton Artists
148-151:	Jared D. Lee
152-153:	John C. Shedd Aquarium*; Hal Just
154-155:	© Monterey Bay Aquarium*
156-157:	© John C. Shedd Aquarium*; Joseph M. Choromanski, Aquarium of the Americas, New Orleans*; Sea World, Inc. (Bob Covey)*
158-159:	© Lynn M. Stone
160-163:	Yoshi Miyake
164-167:	Jean Cassels
168-169:	Eileen Mueller Neill
170-171:	© Norvia Behling*; Andrew Jacks, TSW/Chicago Ltd.*
172-173:	Eileen Mueller Neill; © Norvia Behling*
174-175:	Joan Holub
176-177:	Joan Holub; Hans Keinhard, Okapia from Photo Researchers*; Joan Holub; © St. Meyers, Okapia from Photo Researchers*
178-179:	Joan Holub
180-181:	Eileen Mueller Neill
182-183:	© Tim Davis, Photo Researchers*
184-185:	David Austen, TSW/Chicago Ltd.*; Cameramann International, Ltd.*; © Elisabeth Weiland, Photo Researchers*
186-187:	Cary Wolinsky, Stock Boston; © David R. Frazier, Photo Researchers*
188-189:	Pat & Robin DeWitt
190-191:	Pat & Robin DeWitt; © Leonard Lee Rue III, Photo Researchers*
192-193:	© Mickey Gibson, Animals Animals
194-197:	Yoshi Miyake
198-199:	Fritz Prenzel, TSW/Chicago Ltd.*
200-201:	John Cancalosi*
202-203:	Yoshi Miyake
204-205:	© Sea World, Inc.*
206-207:	Steven D. Mach
208-209:	Steven D. Mach; Betsy Day
210-211:	© Robert Frerck, Odyssey Productions*; Toni Angermayer, Photo Researchers*
212-213:	© Robert Frerck, Odyssey Productions*
214-217:	Steven D. Mach
218-219:	Sea World, Inc. (Geoff Reed)*
220-223:	Paul Meisel
224-225:	© Judy Carter, Wolf Hollow*
226-227:	School of Veterinary Medicine, University of Illinois*; © Judy Carter, Wolf Hollow*
228-233:	Pat & Robin DeWitt
234-235:	Pat & Robin DeWitt; Eileen Mueller Neill
236-239:	Eileen Mueller Neill
240-241:	Eileen Mueller Neill; Illustration by Garth Williams from *Charlotte's Web*, © 1952 HarperCollins Publishers. Reproduced by permission of the publisher*
242-243:	Eileen Mueller Neill
244-251:	Steven D. Mach

Index

This index is an alphabetical list of the important topics covered in this book. it will help you find information given in both words *and* pictures. To help you understand what an entry means, there is sometimes a helping word in parentheses, for example, *aviary* (bird cage). If there is information in both words and pictures, you will see the words *with pictures* after the page number. If there is *only* a picture, you will see the word *picture* after the page number.